MOTHER'S PRISONER

A Memoir

To: Sydna

From: Pam

With Love and a Desire to Inspire.
Happy Reading!

GERALDINE MURRELL-GODFREY

Murrell & Murrell Publications

Mother of A Prisoner
A Memoir
All Rights Reserved.
Copyright © 2018 Geraldine Murrell-Godfrey
v2.0

The opinions expressed in this manuscript are solely the opinions of the author and do not represent the opinions or thoughts of the publisher. The author has represented and warranted full ownership and/or legal right to publish all the materials in this book.

This book may not be reproduced, transmitted, or stored in whole or in part by any means, including graphic, electronic, or mechanical without the express written consent of the publisher except in the case of brief quotations embodied in critical articles and reviews.

Murrell & Murrell Publications

ISBN: 978-0-578-20242-6

Cover Photo © 2018 thinkstockphotos.com. All rights reserved - used with permission.

PRINTED IN THE UNITED STATES OF AMERICA

FOREWORD

THIS BOOK, "MOTHER of A Prisoner", is a riveting, heartwarming, and raw invitation into the worst experience of a mother, whose son wound up in an unlikely place, based upon his middle class, both parents in the home, upbringing, -A prison. G Murrell-Godfrey is poised to be one of the nation's top non-fiction writers. She brings to life, the heart wrenching account of how her "baby boy" was arrested, carted off to a dirty jail cell and then had to await trial and sentencing for over a year and then finally wound up in Prison, with a six (6) year sentence, which some would say did not fit the crime. She teaches us how to lean and depend on God, while gaining an understanding of the harshness of the so-called justice system.

I have known G Murrell-Godfrey all of my life, having met her in elementary school and then attended junior high, high school and also college with Mrs. Godfrey. She has always been a person who was not afraid to express her opinion, regardless of the difficulty of the circumstances. I am now serving my 5th term as Clerk of the Circuit Court of Cook County Illinois, the second largest court system in the United States, so I have a front row seat of the criminal justice system which she brings to life in this book. "Mother of A Prisoner" captures the essence of the woman I know G Murrell-Godfrey to be. She has never shied away from difficult challenges, and with this book, she was not afraid to reveal to the world, a very embarrassing time in her and her family's lives. Many would have hidden this experience, but G Murrell-Godfrey saw the greater good in sharing her experience with us all.

Whether you are a mother, father, sister, brother, child or relative of someone who has been incarcerated or not, this book is for you. This book describes in vivid details, what is going on with the disproportionate minority confinement in our criminal justice system, which was described by Michelle Alexander in her book, as the "New Jim Crow", and theorized by me personally as "Attempted Black Genocide", where blacks are concerned. One of the best ways to reduce or get rid of a race of people is to reduce their opportunities for procreation. Putting potential fathers(Black) in prison, making them felons and then stigmatizing them after release as ineligible to be decent husbands, is in my opinion a way of reducing the rate of population growth of blacks in America, which was evident in the last census. This supports my theory of Black imprisonment as being "Attempted Black Genocide". This book should compel all of us to action and to say YES WE CAN CHANGE; and it should force us to change our perception of the men and women who find themselves in an unfortunate place- A Prison thereby giving their mothers, the 'dishonored badge of being the "Mother of a Prisoner".

Dorothy A. Brown-Cook
Clerk of the Circuit Court of Cook County, Illinois

PRAISE FOR " MOTHER OF A PRISONER"

I believe that God prepared Geraldine during her time as a prison volunteer years before the tumultuous journey that her son endured as an inmate. Her book, "Mother of a Prisoner" chronicles her experience in coping with a suddenly imprisoned son and also provides mental, moral and spiritual support for thousands of other parents in similar situations. This book is a must read, very insightful.

Denise Jackson, Journalist...................Illinois

Geraldine's endeavor to write this book is commendable. This is a story that must be told. Many of us have relatives which have gone through similar situations, but perhaps not to the magnitude as Geraldine has, and definitely not as transparent. "Mother of a Prisoner " tells the story of hundreds of thousands of mothers throughout not only the United States, but throughout the world.

*Samuel Petty, Retiree (**Central Illinois Light Company**)
and Member of Several Civic Boards*

PRAISE FOR "MOTHER OF A PRISONER"

Being a former chaplain at the Illinois Department of Corrections, I have seen the pain of mothers and fathers who have had their sons and daughters incarcerated by their own actions and in some cases falsely accused. These parents have suffered emotionally and financially in trying to defend their child. By the grace of God, He can turn that prison (cemetery) experience into a seminary (religious) awakening for their loved ones. I know that Geraldine's book, "Mother of a Prisoner", will be a help and inspiration to many who have incarcerated loved ones and also to those who are serving time themselves.

Richard Hammonds, Pastor/Founder Gospel Experience Church, Peoria, Illinois

In "Mother of a Prisoner" Murrell-Godfrey gives a captivating account of a mischance that upturned her life. She takes us behind the tears and prayers of a woman who was once a prison volunteer and now must cope with the reality of her eldest son's incarceration in state prison. She succeeds admirably in using her story to delve into the injustices of the American judicial system interpretation and application of the law. This is a 'must read' for anyone concerned about the plight of African American males and the moral direction of this country.

Daphne Jennings, Bachelor of Social Work, former mental health caseworker

TABLE OF CONTENTS

1. Introduction 1
2. A Broken Heart 8
3. My Son, The C R _ _ _ _ _L 14
4. Where Are My Friends? 24
5. My First Jail Visit 30
6. Sentencing Day 35
7. Examining My Feelings 41
8. Entry Denied 55
9. What Shall I Tell My Grandson? 65
10. My Son Is Not a Statistic 74
11. Release Day 82
12. Free But Not Free 89
13. Reality Check vs Tough Love 99
14. Second Chance 103
15. One Year Later 115
16. One On One Interview with My Son, the Former Inmate (FI) 125
17. Dear Son (Response to Interview) 136
18. Where Do We Go From Here –It's Not Your Fault 139
Resources and References 147
Acknowledgements 149
About the Author 151

INTRODUCTION

HOW MANY TIMES have you listened to the news broadcasts and headlines about a young black man who has had a run-in with the law and may have said to yourself or your spouse-"that's too bad, I'm glad that my son has his mind focused and is not involved with whatever or whomever." And so goes the ragging on this young man's obvious plight-and the ragging about where are his parents? How could he do such a thing? Now if you are a true Christian parent, you don't condemn this young man, you would probably make a confession similar to this 'My son will not break the law, nor break his mother's heart, but he will be the man that God has called him to be-in Jesus name, Amen.' That's very admirable of you as a Christian parent—sprinkled with a bit of self-righteousness. Is there anybody within the confines of the local church structure praying for this young man whom you just saw on the evening news? How do you know that he actually is guilty of the alleged crime? Besides, you know his parents-won't you even give them a call? Now this book is not just for Christians, it is for anybody that has a loved one who is currently incarcerated or someone who knows a family that has a member behind bars. It is also for those who really care about the increasingly number of black males who are doing time and try to understand what the driving force behind this recurring trend is and the effect on the family left behind.

If you are just a regular parent who saw that same news clip you may respond something like this 'now that boy needs some guidance' and you might say 'real men don't do things like that'. You may even take an extreme position by grabbing your adolescent son and pointing him to the television set and daring him to never do anything so stupid otherwise he'll be on the evening news also. Do you remember the theme song for the television detective named Baretta—"if you can't do the time –then don't do the crime". We all have our ways of getting our children's attention-some of them actually work and some do more harm.

My response was more geared to the lack of parental oversight—spoken like a true middle-class parent, right? I have no sisters, only one brother and I am proud to say that he did not go astray. My father was in the home. It was the four of us-father, mother, brother and myself—a perfect sized family in a small northwest Louisiana town. My father only had a sixth grade education but he was very good in math. I remember to this day, that I had problems doing the conversions—quarts to gallons, pecks and bushels, ounces to pounds. As a matter of fact my father had to assist me when I was in elementary school on this very topic. He would grab a pencil and start figuring things out with that left hand-determined to help his baby girl out. I miss my dad so much. We lost him to cancer in 1994.

"Mother of a Prisoner" was born out of a true experience—mine, one I do not wish for any parent to go through regardless of race or class. Perhaps you have heard or read about the high incidence of incarceration of black males in the judicial system –this was not supposed to happen to MY son.

The sociologists, educators, psychologists and the like have practically forecast what the future looks like (according to their data) for hundreds of our young black males-but not My Son. Now in 2015, we had some unexpected support from Congress from some senators and representatives about incarceration and our judicial system with regards to African Americans.

My son was different, he has my DNA. My son has a son. I never bought into this theory that 80% of our young black males between the ages of 18-35 will most likely end up in jail or prison. My husband and I are both college graduates and we have worked very hard.

INTRODUCTION

We both have had our share of experiences with racism on the job, off the job as well as unpleasant dealings with all kinds of people.

Those experiences did not end up in the courts. We have always tried to make a difference in this world which is what you do especially if you graduated from a HBCU (historical black colleges and universities). Neither of our parents finished high school.

I am just as proud as any other mother who has birthed 2 special young men to carry on the family's name and to reach their fullest potential by being the men of God that the Lord has destined for each of them to be.

So what-one of them took a detour to his destiny. Just because a person takes a detour does not necessarily mean that they will not reach their destination. It merely means that their arrival time has been deferred. Consider it in the context of an airline flight. My flight number 5663 from Dallas to St. Louis has been delayed due to bad weather in St. Louis. This flight has been rescheduled for a later departure time and consequently a later arrival time. It will get to St. Louis but not at my initial desired date or time. The question is how do I occupy my time during this delayed departure? Do I sit around and watch the amusing people you see running through the airports to catch their flights or do I pull out my cell phone and call some friends or do I take out that book that I've been reading for weeks now or lastly do I take out my 'Write It Down' tablet and do just that. Well I have been delayed on flights before and have managed to do all of the above.

This book is dedicated to every mother that has sat where I am sitting and to every parent that has wondered 'how could this have happened to me?' Perhaps you feel like I felt-- that you have been blindsided. It is my intention to be as transparent as possible with hopes that this book will dispel such misinformation that the lack of good parenting and the absence of a father in the home is a breeding ground for future inmates-Not True. As you try to decipher my feelings on these upcoming pages and chapters, perhaps you will either say I never knew it involved all of this or you might say I know exactly what she is going through. We are definitely going to have a discussion about our children that have landed on the inside of the fence- our nation's jails and prisons. People forget that prisoners are people too. They are our sons, daughters, nephews, uncles, cousins, husbands, aunts, sisters, brothers, parents and even our grandchildren.

It has taken me a period of seven plus years to complete this story because I am sharing with you all that I have been going through since 2005-the arrest of my oldest son. The actual trial and eventual sentence did not occur until approximately fifteen months later which is when my son started his six year prison sentence at an Illinois state prison, nearly 1000 miles from Texas, and our new home. Please note that some chapters are written during the present tense while my son was actually incarcerated and what this period was like for me as well as during the parole period. From time to time I will speak in the past tense of what I experienced as well as what I am experiencing today. Be prepared for the changing tone of my voice on these pages which occurred over a seven year plus period.

During his years of incarceration, I reminded my son that his temporary state of imprisonment is likened unto a transformation chamber. In one of my letters I told him to let the Lord transform him while he was in this inside chamber. You may think that I am trying to sound like a psychologist with that analogy, au contraire'. I was just being a spirit-filled mother who looks for a God opportunity in practically everything. This is how I have lived my life over the past three plus decades. Had I not had a stable walk with the Lord, this thing would have destroyed me. Oh, but by the grace and mercy of God, I made it through. Hallelujah. Praise the Lord.

Because it has taken me some time to get all of my collected thoughts together, as you read this book, I will from time to time speak in the present (post-prison term) and in the past(during prison).

You will get a chance to hear from those closest to me, how this incident affected them, in their own words. I will expose the feelings of hopelessness, embarrassment, anger, disappointment and a feeling of how the heck did this thing get in my bloodline? Let's take a sneak

INTRODUCTION

peek at one of the feelings that I will delve into later—the feeling of disappointment. How could this have happened to me? In the religious circle, I am known as Sister Godfrey. I was an active member of two prison ministry teams for about seven years. During that time of prison ministry, my son was for the most part, still living at home even though he had finished high school and had taken some college courses. My son knew that I was in prison ministry, how could he ultimately end up in the one place that I was trying to spread some hope to those fellows who were imprisoned already. Was he not paying attention?! You never know where the road of life with its various highways, curves and roadside ditches will take you. One word of advice-Be Ready.

You will find out by sharing this experience with me that statistics are not always accurate and all persons of the same ethnic group do not end up in the same place or do they have the same values. In life THINGS HAPPEN. I have read one statistic which states that over 90% of the young black males incarcerated do not have a high school diploma or GED. Another report states that most young black men incarcerated come from a single parent households-wrong again. Statistics would also have you believe that young black males who end up in the judicial system have fathers who are already or have been in the system-wrong again. My son is not a STATISTIC.

Before we departed for Texas, I met with my son and laid my hands on his forehead and told him to protect the family name. In less than eight months of us selling the home that we had lived in for 19 years and moving across country, I received a call that my son has been picked up by the police. I shouted "What?" Who do you call when you are a thousand miles away-to stand proxy for you with your son who has just been arrested?

My husband and I had already moved to Texas while my son was being arrested, charged, and made to sleep on a dirty jailhouse floor because of the lack of beds and having to share the same nasty toilet as others while eating suspenseful food. My youngest son was in law school in St. Louis at this time. Who would be my proxy to go visit my son, put money on the books, assure him that we will do all that we can to get him out as soon as we can? At this juncture in my life, I felt that I was being put to the test to see if I, myself, believed all that I had been saying to the young men whom we had ministered to for years in the prisons in central Illinois. As a group we did bi-monthly trips to the prisons to spread some hope, cheer, shook hands and prayed with several inmates for reduced terms and some wanted prayer for early parole. Some young men shared with us that we were the only visitors that they received.

They stated that because some had repeated offenses that their families had given up on them and no longer visited them. Can you even imagine that? A person is already locked up and because they came back through that awful prison revolving door, their families have given up and no longer visit that individual. According to my son, this happens more often than one would imagine. Perhaps this is one reason for the rage that sometimes runs rampant within any prison. Your family has given up and cast you out of their lives.

I will share the heartbreak, my tears and what I did to keep it all together. Besides, this young man looks like me and my late father. He's tall, slender, easy going and now has just made a bad choice that possibly may affect him for the rest of his life. He has my DNA; he is not supposed to be in prison. He has a toddler aged son-of whom he will miss the formative years. His brother is a young attorney; he can't be sitting up in a prison. What the heck happened?

We had lived in Illinois for nearly 30 years when we decided to move back South where it's warmer and closer to our aging parents. My son then decides to play the prison card! Why he was sanctified in my womb, both of my sons were and as well as my daughter, who suffocated while in the care of a babysitter over thirty years ago. This was a different type of heartbreak and a whole different ordeal which will be shared in my next book. He was supposed to be a construction engineer. He does not have time to sit in jail nor in prison! Now you have to labor with and against the Illinois State judicial system. My husband and I are not making the kind of money that we once made

INTRODUCTION

which would now limit our return trips back and forth to Illinois, not to mention legal fees. With both of our sons grown and out of the house, we are now empty nesters—we were definitely blindsided by this incident.

This was a very difficult story to write mainly because I am living it every day and have been now for about seven years. You will travel with me from the moment I received that phone call on to me sending money to put on the books for my son, on to driving him back and forth to Fort Worth for 12 weeks for substance abuse (which was not a part of his life) and anger management classes all required as conditions of his parole. I hope that my words frame and express my feelings through all of the no's he received on job applications and the embarrassment of having actually started a job and having the floor manager come tap him on the shoulder and escort him out of an employment location. The upper management said No after the background check came through. Note that my son did declare his criminal background on the application. His hurt was my hurt—even though I was not present with him at the time of these disappointments-I felt his pain-his embarrassment.

In no way am I trying to minimize my son's criminal actions or glamorize what my family has gone through. During this story you will feel my pain and my shame. You may not see the cloud which hovered over my brain continually as I try to figure out and even reason how did this thing happen to us? Afterwards, you straighten up, hold your head up and begin to count the days, the months and the years until your child or love one comes back home. I am not so naïve to think that every person reading this book will joyfully and soon be reunited with their loved ones. I will say this 'with God all things are possible and nothing is impossible'. I will repeat the following statement many times throughout this book because it is a fundamentally true fact—in life-THINGS HAPPEN.

I am the Mother of a Prisoner and this is my story.

A BROKEN HEART

FOR MONTHS NOW we were told by our son's lawyer that the district attorney had a weak case. Our attorney was banking his defense for our son on the fact that the young lady had actually invited our son over to her home and then sometimes during the evening before he arrived-she had changed her mind. He was the attorney, the professional, so we relied totally on his expertise. Upon my son's ultimate arrival to her house(he had a habit of not being anywhere on time), she had decided that she no longer wanted to see him that night and refused to answer the front door when he rang the bell.

Her refusal to open the door did upset my son. First and foremost I want you to know that this young lady is not the mother of my grandson. As a matter of fact, I have never met her and would not recognize her if she rang our door bell today. I am not even sure when her and my son became an item. Like any decent mother/grandmother you wished for your son to join himself again with the mother of his child. Why did they have to break-up? Why couldn't they remain a family? This whole thing is just heartbreaking. I've lost one child, my firstborn in death while in the care of a babysitter, now must I lose my second born to the judicial system. Is there any parent reading this that can relate to what this sort of life changing incident can do to your emotions? It is almost like being sucker punched right in the heart with no time to recover from the hit.

I am sharing a lot of background information so that anyone reading this may say "this happened to a friend of mine or a family member of mine or it happened to me". Life is not fair. It certainly does not ease the heartbreak by me being nearly 1000 miles away from my imprisoned son. If we were still in Illinois then I would be able to visit him more frequently.

Another reason that my heart was shattered is that this son looks the most (out of my two boys) like me—tall, dark and handsome (in my case attractive). I knew he had a bit of a temper but I did not know he would actually knock in somebody's front door. Now tell me –how well do you know your child? At the time of this incident, my son was delivering pizza and making small financial contributions toward the welfare of his son to the baby's mother. He had been away from school for about 3 semesters and was glad to be back in and was looking forward to finally completing his Associates degree and graduating.

Prior to even the thought of leaving Illinois, I had spoken with my son countless times about him not spending enough quality time with his son, little Theo, my grandson. My son, TJ, is a young man full of vigor, incredibly smart yet with a generous dose of irresponsibility. As his mother I knew he wasn't ready to become a father at the age of 23-but nonetheless-surprise he told me that I'm going to be a grandmother in 30 days. Seriously? Yes, seriously and it was indeed so. This revelation came about when we had not heard from him in several weeks and he was not returning my voice messages. So being concerned I went by his apartment and left a 'motherly' note underneath his door assured to get a response. The next day he surfaced with a late night phone call of me becoming a grandmother in 30 days. It may have been late but I still recalled that it takes nine months to deliver a baby-in most pregnancies. This joyous announcement regardless how uncanny it was delivered—was definitely not a heartbreak moment. For my grandson is the spitting image of my now incarcerated son.

Prior to my husband and me actually departing for Texas I had a talk with my son and with my grandson's mother. When we left Illinois my grandson was nearly 18 months old. I encouraged my son to spend as much time as he could with little Theo.

We were now official members of the Empty Nesters club-all children out of the home. Son number one remained in Illinois with his son nearby. Son number two had graduated from college and getting ready to enter the Masters program and attend law school. Everything was moving along just fine. It was within the first eight months after getting settled in a new city and state, we received a shocking phone call late in the afternoon from one of our son's friends that our son, TJ, had been arrested on breaking into his girlfriend's apartment. What? We knew the mother of his son lived in a house, who in the heck was in an apartment? We were stunned and baffled. We were in the car when the call came in from Illinois and I started to hyperventilate. What just happened? How credible was the bearer of the news? Who do we call if our son is arrested? Time stood still until we made it home but my head was still spinning and my heart still racing after receiving this shocking news. How can this be happening to our family? Heck, I was an active member of two prison ministry groups for 7 years! How can my son be facing prison? We're in the midst of buying a home here in Texas—how can this be happening? Not now! Oh my God. I could hardly speak for the remainder of the evening but was in fervent prayer. My emotions skyrocketed-my heart was breaking, my head started hurting-and we had to settle down to figure out if the information was at all accurate.

Since I knew that arrests records were put in the local paper generally the next day afterwards, we of course went to the website of the local newspaper. There it was- in plain sight for the entire city of Peoria to see—listed along with twenty-five other arrests was our son's name, his age-25, his address and with these charges listed: home invasion, criminal trespass to a residence and domestic battery. These charges combined carry a sentence of up to 30 years. The date of that newspaper article was May 23, 2005 which I printed from the internet and still holding on to it to this day. As you read this, you have no idea how this made my husband and me feel. Mind you that my son carries my husband's name. Perhaps people that knew us would at a glance think it was my husband's name listed in the newspaper until you factor in the age of course.

After getting a fragmented version from his friend of what lead to our son's arrest, we were in shock while in the vehicle all the way back home. My husband was furious-how could TJ get himself in such a predicament-with my name, he says? I have several friends who subscribe to the local paper and religiously review the arrest record section---no one contacted us at all. With a sir name as ours and me being in the public light for several years prior—at the time of this publication—even though we had left town—it was still soon enough for a person to dial our old number and immediately be given our new phone number.

Didn't anybody care? I believe the local phone company makes that information available for up to 1 year after a person has vacated their previous phone number. This type of hurt will be covered in a later chapter entitled "Where are my friends?" I am a godly woman, I have always been an active member of a local church during the thirty years of living in Illinois and most of all I had been faithful in prison ministry. My son could very well be headed to prison. How could this have happened? This shocking news grips you suddenly; you don't know who to call. I was stuttering mentally inside. Once home I had to actually lie down so I could think. Definitely since you're all the way in Texas—who should you call?? He and I had a conversation about protecting the family name before we pulled up stakes and left Illinois. Why would he wait until we have moved all the way across country, in another state—and subject himself to a stunt like this? Right now if I sound furious—well reality is setting in and I am furious! I'm just not so sure whom I am more furious at—my son, that girl, the law, myself or just at life!

In life you will find out that there are many surprises good and bad alike, that will test your resolve and you will discover what is really on the inside of you. There are so many emotions that are going on in our family right now, particularly in me, which I cannot enumerate at this time. You may be an individual who think you have it all together—but if you have ever received such a phone call or maybe yours is forth coming, just keep on reading. The truth be told, my heart had been broken into pieces just based on the news itself. I cannot fathom what will happen next. We have never been down this road before. Where is the 'what to do when you child has been arrested' guide and is facing serious charges and you are not in the upper income bracket and you're not a celebrity where sometimes, not all the times, money can make certain charges disappear. What do you do? Just keep reading.

I am the Mother of a Prisoner and this is my story.

September 30, 2006

Dear Friend(s),

Our hearts have been broken. In case you were not aware, our oldest son, T.J. was recently found guilty of serious charges involving his former girlfriend. We are asking you to join with us by writing a letter to the judge asking for leniency for our son. Our son is not a dangerous person and did no harm to this young lady. Some items in her apartment did get broken. He did make a bad error in judgment by going into her apartment. Our son is facing serious prison time and that is why we are asking for your help. T.J. is now 27 years old and has a 3 year old son (our grandson, Theo). T.J. was within 12 hours of getting an Associate Degree in Construction Engineering at Illinois Central College prior to this situation. He was going to school during the day and delivering pizza at night. We know that he must be held accountable for his action-we just ask for leniency-which is what any parent would ask for. We pray that when the judge pronounces sentence on November 3rd, that he would take into consideration that this is our son's first conviction and he is not dangerous. This situation was a lover's quarrel. Please note that this young woman is not the mother of our grandson. T.J. wants to finish his education and help raise his son. If you are comfortable in saying something to this effect please do so on the enclosed paper and sign and date your letter. Everything you need has been provided for you in this packet as we know that you are busy with your own lives. Don't forget to put your return address on the envelope so the delivery to the judge won't be delayed. Time is of the essence.

If at all possible, please try and mail your letter to the judge within 1 week after you receive this packet. We are thanking God in advance for those of you who are praying for T.J. and us and will take the time to write a note. If you can take 20 minutes to draft a note and mail it, it would mean so much to our family. Thank you.

If you have any questions for us, please call us at our home in Arlington, Texas xxx-xxx-xxxx.

Again, we thank you dearly for standing with us during this trying time.

Mr. & Mrs. Theodore Godfrey

Arlington , Texas (30 years residents of Peoria)

(This was the actual letter I sent to 34 friends and family asking them to join with us in requesting (leniency for our son.)

Mother of a Prisoner

MY SON, THE C R _ _ _ _ L

IT IS VERY difficult for me to refer to my own son as a 'criminal' which is why that word is left with letters missing in the table of contents and in the chapter's title. Just because a person has been found guilty by a jury or by a judge in a bench trial and has been sentenced to a penal institution does this automatically make an individual a criminal? In light of the recent national outcry over the verdict in the 2013 George Zimmerman trial, justice in this country is perceived to be very biased and inconsistent when it comes to mandating sentences for African American citizens and against African American victims. This is especially noticeable among our young men in comparison to individuals of other races for like offenses. A later chapter covers this in greater depth.

If you had heard firsthand the comments spoken by the sentencing judge in my son's case when summarizing the vast letters of support and appeal for leniency from friends and family across the country , you too would agree –"Now what could this aspiring young man have done to deserve this sentence?" Before you form any conclusions and say well she is just the grieving mother of another incarcerated young black man painting a rose-colored canvass about her son-this, is not the case. Those individuals who submitted letters for leniency knew my son and knew how he was raised. I never told anyone what words to say other than a sincere request for leniency. At the time of sentencing my grandson was only 3 years old and was in the courtroom asleep in his mother's lap unaware of what was going on with his dad's life.

The dictionary defines a criminal as one guilty of a crime-usually of a serious nature and one who is wicked. My son did not commit a serious crime. No one was injured let alone killed in this offense. My son definitely is not a 'wicked 'person. You are probably saying there goes a mother 'covering again' for her son. My son stands 6'2" and weighs about 205 pounds. He is chocolate brown complexion like me; with a deep voice and quick wit. He is shy until he gets to know you. He is able to handle himself in any setting which would make him a real people person. He definitely has my personality.

This chapter is probably one of the most challenging to put into words as my son is currently incarcerated at a state prison in Illinois. Keep in mind that in my current job as a housing counselor, the clientele which we serve are homeless persons with disabilities. Many of these individuals have criminal records and a large percentage of them, not all, have spent time in a penal institution or county jail. It tears at my heart to refer to my son as an inmate or as society calls a 'CR_ _ _ _ _L'. When I counsel younger individuals who are seeking housing, I cannot help but think about my son's temporary plight in custody of the Illinois Department of Corrections.

It is every parent's desire to have their child finish high school, go on to college , get a decent job, develop their career and if and when the opportunity presents itself to start their own business. Experts say that some parents whose careers or lives did not reach their fullest expectations, try to re-live their lives through the lives of their child. We encouraged our younger son to explore being a doctor or lawyer at a young age. Upon reaching his senior year in high school finishing with a GPA over 4.0, he even explored studying music professionally. I am not sure what changed his mind, but I am glad that he did. Our youngest son recently graduated from law school, received an additional master's degree in Health Administration and passed the Illinois Bar Exam on the first try.

By way of comparison, one son is a brand new attorney and the other son is doing time. Same DNA, same parents, same upbringing-but my older son decided to take a detour. You may share our sentiment, that the child who took a detour is still my son (daughter).

Just recently I have been glued to the television watching the cable TV show "Lockup", a documentary series on MSNBC, to better understand what goes on inside the prisons. These shows are educational and give enlightenment and sometimes fear to parents like us, or anyone interested in and perhaps seeing where help is needed in this aspect of correctional facilities. Hardly ever is there any coverage about the family of the incarcerated person. That is the reason why I had to write this book. There are many persons who have been incarcerated, did their time and have put their stories in print. Now it is the family's time, in my case, the prisoner's mother, to tell my story.

After surviving the initial arrest of my oldest son (which happened less than eight months after we moved to Texas) and the bench trial in which the judge made his ruling, the second most hurtful piece of this ordeal was the actual Sentencing Day. This is a separate chapter in itself.

When you see your own son, whom you bore and reared into a young man, being escorted into the court room in shackles by the deputies with his hands and feet shackled together in a way that had him bent over as he walked, you have no idea how I felt then. The compelling part about that scene is that as I am writing this particular part of my story, that visual is forever seared in my mind and tears begin again to stream down my face. All of your insides stand still in disbelief. I wanted so much to wail out loud in the courtroom, but I did not want my son to feel any worse than he did already. I said to myself "this is my son in shackles of whom right now I am not pleased." How could he ruin his life? This was very demeaning for me seeing him like that and I can only imagine how he must have felt. My Lord God, this is real life! There's no pinching myself to wake up—I am there in the court room as a supporter and observer of my son's sentencing. You begin to accept the fact that by the world's system and standards, this day my son is considered a CR_ _ _ _ _ L. Parents, family members, trust me; it is still hard to this day to refer to him as a former C R_ _ _ _ _L

The bible teaches us that if any man be in Christ, he is a new creature; old things are passed away and behold all things are become new (II Cor. 5:17) I would not have made it through this ordeal if it had not been for the Word of God and my relationship with Jesus. The puzzling part is that just a few short years prior to my son's offense he was a part of a street outreach team who (along with other brethren) witnessed to hard core individuals on the streets of Chicago about the love of Christ. Now as he's headed to prison he must now draw upon that same 'living water 'which he was offering to others. Just thinking about that part of my son's past, I know he will be alright. He has drunk of that living water himself and I know he will be alright-in Jesus' name.

Of course you've seen the old black and white movies and comedy shows alike, where the prisoners were in black and white stripes. This was no comedy; it was real and there my son, tall, dark still handsome yet broken, standing there dressed in the standard black and white prison garb on. I was yet grasping the fact that this was really happening to my family, to my son- to me! Oh dear God.

I consider myself an emotionally and spiritually strong woman and if I might say so-'quite intelligent' who has been given a godly charisma with practically all kinds of people. This whole ordeal with my son's prison incarceration is unchartered waters for me-for my whole family. My husband attended the bench trial and he called me with the news. His words were "baby, it was so brief, perhaps we should have opted for a jury trial." As a matter of fact, my son's attorney was silent on why or why we should not settle for a bench trial. In hindsight, we should have insisted that he give some recommendation as to the type of trial we should select- he left the decision solely up to us. What we did was what any person would have done— to google 'bench trial' on the internet. My younger son had not been on his job very long and his firm dealt with civil cases not criminal cases. At the same time my husband and I reasoned that because a young lady was involved in this incident, we felt that with a jury trial, the jurors might be more sympathetic toward the female than towards our son so we wanted to protect him from outside judgments. We also thought that the judge would not be biased versus potential female jurors might take exception with our son and render a biased verdict.

One thing that frustrated me with my son-yes-he's in prison-yes I'm his mother and yes some of the things that he was supposed to do before the bench trial-he did not do! Once my husband put up the bail money $5000, my son was to return to work, save all the money he could so he could get an attorney. We were in Texas and he was in Illinois alone, out on bail. He had approximately ten months to work-save – contact various attorneys and take advantage of free consultations to tell his story of what happened and ultimately select an attorney. He did not fulfill his part! How frustrating. So what happened at the 9th hour we were forced to enter into an agreement for representation with a defense attorney referred to him by his son's mother's father. Seriously! We did not know at the time that this defense attorney whom we only knew (after the assignment of the bail money) that he sometimes serves as a public defender. You probably see where this is headed.

My son waited until we sold our home, pulled up stakes and moved 1000 miles away, to get into trouble with the law. Only so much can be done long distance, especially when you're waiting to actually meet with attorneys, review their credentials, where they went to law school, see how professional they are and how you're treated. Your mind is rushing, your heart is racing, you've been praying, so you look up toward heaven and say these two words- "Help Lord!"

There were approximately 6 weeks between the bench trial and the actual sentencing day. The bench trial was held September 13, 2006 and my son would be sentenced on November 3rd. Again feeling underrepresented by our defense counsel, we were still hoping that our son would be released at the bench trial –because our attorney led us to believe that the charges being brought were weak –so we were eager with anticipation. Boy, were we wrong! As a matter of fact, according to my husband, my son showed up to court,

MY SON, THE C R _ _ _ _ L

dressed nicely in regular street clothes, but after the judge's decision, the deputies took him into custody straight from the court room. My son himself was surprised that he was taken into custody. I was not in town for this, but would be coming for the sentencing. My son was facing 30 years for an offense where no one was hurt or killed. Due to the numerous trips we made back and forth to Illinois from Texas in an eighteen month period, we had to alternate travel trips as it became increasingly more expensive.

As a result of that one day bench trial, the judge pronounced my son guilty of the charges of home invasion, criminal trespassing and domestic battery. Yes- those charges sound terrible, but I assure you that this was nothing more than a lover's quarrel. My son was supposed to be over his' then' girlfriend's apartment at a certain time one evening, but he did not show up until hours later. She apparently had grown tired and decided it was too late for company. When he did finally show up, she refused to open the door. This made him angry and he was determined to have their date night, so without thinking and after knocking on the door and ringing the doorbell for several minutes, he decided to knock in her front door which startled this young lady. Yes that's all he did. When he came inside, she was on the phone with someone else, so of course he suspected that she was talking with another guy. I have no idea to this day who this young lady was speaking to nor would I recognize her if she knocked on my door today. They tussled over the phone; he broke some items inside her apartment, after which he left. There were no weapons involved at all. She called the police and filed a report. It took a whole year for his case to come to trial.

Because we endured that one day bench trial instead of a jury trial and the judge's pronouncement of guilt, my son is officially regarded as a 'criminal' by society's standards. He was not born a CR _ _ _ _ _ L was not reared to be a CR_ _ _ _ _ L, nor did he attend college to become a CR_ _ _ _ _L. For a split second he took his eyes off of his future and made a terrible decision which rewarded him the unpopular distinction of being referred to as a criminal.

MOTHER OF A PRISONER

Every day I wade through my feelings-my feelings of being brokenhearted, embarrassment, and disappointment and outraged. Sometimes it feels like a bad dream. So much so that I want to wake up and dream something else. Not so. This is really happening.

How could my son do this to me? Yes, I said it—how could he do this to' me? ' I am a woman of God, a college graduate, a professional woman, one who did not bear any children out of wedlock. How could he do this to me? I have never been on any kind of public assistance, never lived in subsidized housing, repaid my school loan, achieved the title of Realtor of the year of a Midwestern city—how could he do this to me?? I was a former Director at a local housing agency and most of all I was a member of the prison ministry team for 7 years—I ministered to inmates and now' my ' own son has a 6 digit number by which he is identified by within the Illinois Department of Corrections. I know this number well R57102. Every piece of mail, money order, magazine, newspaper –everything had to have his number placed on it otherwise he would probably not receive it or receive it much later with just the inmates' name only. This happens when you are incarcerated—you LOSE YOUR FREEDOM! You lose your identity and are given a number. The prison officials refer to you by that 6 digit number. I do realize in other states it may be longer than 6 digits. Actually my son's number contained one alphabet and 5 numerals.

We had already made the move to Texas when my son was arrested for this charge. As best I can recall, this incident happened on a Tuesday or a Wednesday and my son was picked up later in the week while on a pizza delivery run. Yes—he was working. So he had on his work uniform, the pizza or whatever food item he was delivering—the pizza company's money bag and of course his car was left at the customer's residence—until a friend was able to come get it. This in itself is embarrassing and unfortunately this scene has been played out on television many times where the accused is picked up and placed under arrest at their place of employment. Speaking as the mother, my son was not supposed to have been the person arrested

MY SON, THE C R _ _ _ _ _L

while doing an honest day's work. Not my son! My son should have never knocked in that girl's front door or anyone's front door when the invitation had been withdrawn. This would change his life forever. Additionally, this would also change MY life forever. He is not the only person who has taken a detour on the way to his destiny. It doesn't mean you won't necessarily reach your destiny--your arrival time has definitely been delayed by this detour.

According to the law, my son became a "CR_ _ _ _AL " at the age of 25 years old and spent his 26th, 27th, 28th and 29th birthdays locked up in an Illinois prison. As his birthday approached every year, I pondered and wondered how my son was handling being behind bars especially on the twenty-sixth birthday (the first one spent behind bars) He received at least three or four birthday cards each year. One from his grandmother (my mom), his son's mother, his brother and of course one from me. During his time behind bars a couple of my friends did volunteer and send him a birthday card or two which meant a lot to our family.

One generally thinks of a criminal as a depraved individual who has no feelings, no goals who just wants to take from others and never giving back. This is not the case with my son and that's why I will never refer to him as a " CR _ _ _ _ _L".

I'd like to pose this question: when does a person stop being referred to as a 'criminal'? An individual does his or her time, pays their debt to society and the world refuses to let them move on- constantly being reminded of their past wrongdoing(s). There is also a segment of society which brands parents of criminals-even when the offender has been released. When does it stop?

Treating others the way I want to be treated is the Golden Rule and my personal mantra. This is why I had no problem in joining the prison ministry team years before this incident. I consider myself a mature Christian and have found my calling-ministering to persons behind bars. This calling also includes speaking life and encouragement to the discouraged. People need to feel that they matter and this is what I do. Not one time during my seven years as a part of the prison ministry team did it enter into my mind or my heart that one day my 'own' son would end up in a prison facility?

The first time which I was able to visit my son behind bars was when he was still an inmate at the county jail awaiting his actual sentencing. The hours of visitation at the county jail were limited to evenings, two days during the week at a limited time block and on Saturday mornings. If you expected to visit someone during the evening hours you had to arrive at the facility around 6 or 6:30 pm to sign in and then wait in the crowded wait area with limited seating. I recall during my one and only visit which was on Halloween night, some of the people in the wait area looked as if they themselves should have been on the other side of the wall instead of the visiting side. Sorry, that's just the way I saw it. Did I for one moment forget that I, too, was there to see an inmate? No- I didn't because 'my' son was not supposed to be in there—so give me a break—reality had not set in on me at that time. I did not know that soon and very soon reality would hit me like a ton of bricks. Oh my, my son is a " CR _ _ _ _L!" Really?! What happened?

While visiting an inmate at the county jail you were not allowed to wear coats or jackets nor could you take any purses. Tonight being a cold Halloween evening, that meant everything had to be locked in your vehicle and your car keys were given to the jailer at the front window. Your keys were tagged and you were given a receipt for them. I remember waiting about 2 hours before my son's name was called and then was only given about 20 minutes to talk to my son on a phone behind a glass window (just like you see on television) This was the first time that I had seen my son in eighteen months and he was in a place where I never dreamed of seeing either one of my boys. I sat down on a small stool on the opposite side of a finger printed dirty glass window waiting for my son to come to the area. I was crying inside but I did not want him to see me cry. I did not want him to see how much he had broken my heart. All the plans that I had for him and had hoped for him—we were just blindsided as a family. I had to calm myself down inwardly and be presentable

MY SON, THE C R _ _ _ _ L

as a strong caring mother anxiously waiting to see her incarcerated son. I had to be strong (for him) because my son had to be having a hard enough time waiting to be sentenced the next day. And besides I was a God fearing woman- a professional woman, former Realtor of the year, former Department Director, former board member and here I sit at the Peoria County jail waiting to see my oldest son-who is now known by the world's standard as a "CRI_ _ _ _ L. Pardon me. I am still to this day grappling with the fact that my son at this time is considered as such.

You have no idea how hard it was for me to accept this reference to my child (I don't care if he was a full grown man) I birthed him so therefore he is my child. Someone once said that if you're an alcoholic- you must first accept it before you can denounce it. A person must first admit that they are lost before they seek out help to be found. A person must also admit their incompetence before they accept help in becoming competent in any given area. The correlation goes on and on—but Not In This Case. My son in the eyes of his BIGGEST supporter, me, his mother, will never be seen as a CRI_ _ _ _ L. The Bible declares that as a man thinketh in his heart-so is he (Proverbs 23:7). I can also assure you that as a mother declares—so it is with her son.

I am the Mother of a Prisoner and this is my story.

WHERE ARE MY FRIENDS?

AS THESE DAYS go by and the time for my son's sentencing grows near, I now pause and ask 'Where are my friends?" I cannot believe that my Christian sisters and brothers have not called me in Texas while all of this hit the papers back in Peoria. Just the other weekend I mailed out 34 personal letters to friends and family members asking them to send letters of petition to the judge requesting leniency on behalf of my son. That exact letter appeared in the previous chapter.

I shared with them that my heart had been broken and the fact that my son is facing serious jail time based on the charges. Knowing that people have their own lives, I made it easy for them by enclosing a pre-addressed stamped envelope to the judge overseeing my son's case. They would still have to write their letter, sign it and mail it to the county court house. In fairness to them I did include a short summary describing the charges which my son had been accused of and found guilty of during the bench trial. I enclosed my home number in the event that someone wanted to ask me questions about the whole ordeal. One person from Illinois did call me about the circumstances surrounding the events which led to my son being incarcerated in the first place. This shows that this brother had honest reservations, which I can respect. He was also a prison team member of ours. Before he wrote and signed anything he wanted to be clear about a few facts. My answers satisfied him and he promised to send a letter requesting leniency. I don't know how many of them actually took the time to write a note, but based on the judge's response to the letters of support, most of them did respond to which I am truly grateful. My high school class president even responded to my e-mail plea and agreed to also send a letter to the judge on Monday morning.

The bible says that if a man wants friends he must first show himself friendly, which is what I did for thirty years as a resident of Central Illinois. Like anyone else, I had my inner circle of friends; at least I thought I did. The inner circle of friends were those persons who have seen you without wigs, weave and also without make-up. The inner circle have seen and heard you cry. They may have even heard you use a curse word and immediately repent. The inner circle were the ones who confided in you when they couldn't pay their bills and those whom you have prayed for God to send them a mate. The inner circle were with you when you prayed and asked God for something and God said 'no' they stood with you anyhow, not knowing that you had already heard from God.

Where were they at a time when our family's personal business was listed in the local newspaper? Where are my friends? My son's bench trial was on September 13, 2006 and he would be sentenced on November 3, 2006. My husband flew in from Texas to sit in on the bench trial and I would be flying back for the actual sentencing day. Neither one of us knew what to expect. The scripture that I harbored in my heart particularly as I awaited the sentencing was Proverbs 21:1; which states that "the king's heart is in the hand of the Lord as the rivers of water; he turneth it whithersoever He will. In our case, the king's position was equal to the judge's position—they both have power, however the ultimate power rests in the hand of the Lord. I believed it and hence that is how I prayed. Perhaps you would have taken a different route, which would certainly be your prerogative. In the case of my inner circle of friends, NO ONE CALLED!

I did receive an e-mail the morning which my son's name appeared in the police record section of the local newspaper. This really hurt. I lived in that city for 30 years and had not been gone 12 months and nobody recognized our last name? Seriously? I was in the public eye for years. The last church of which I was a member prior to moving to Texas, a relatively small congregation—no one called either. God bless them, they came over and helped us pack and load that oversize U-Haul truck back in 2004—but less than twelve months—as a matter of fact it was eight months exactly from our departure date that my son was arrested. Why aren't my friends as well as my last church congregation which I was an active member of calling me and telling me-"Sister we saw it in the paper and we're praying for you? " That did not happen. I did not want pity—just support from the sisters and brothers. Where are my friends?

In this average size central Illinois town, the funny thing is that we were the only African American family with the sir name as ours. Besides for sixteen years I was in the public eye in real estate and a lot of people recognized my name. Subsequent to real estate, I had also been one of the department heads at the local housing authority and had served on one of the city's advisory commissions and local boards. I said that to say this, no matter what income bracket you were in, either me or the company which I worked for probably had a direct or indirect transaction with you if you were in the market any time during my sixteen years in real estate. Quite possibly you would recognize my name if you had been a landlord during my latter years in Peoria. I had one of those names that people remembered. So what if we had moved and if they called and perhaps got a recording—one thing for sure I believe the phone company automatically would refer callers to our old local number to the new number in Texas for up to a year. I am seriously taken aback that none of the persons on the prison ministry teams which I served alongside-none of them bothered to call initially. They were faithful subscribers of the local newspaper so shouldn't they have seen that entry under the crime section with our sir name listed?

I am going to stop now and offer this prayer because I need it-Father, please forgive me if I am thinking of myself more highly than I OUGHT but the people in the central Illinois Christian dome community-especially the African American congregations are pretty close knit about things like this. I need your help in forgiving them because it hurts so badly; in Jesus name Amen.

My husband kept telling me to get over it and leave those people alone—that out of sight is out of mind. Do most men feel that way? Besides we had only moved about 1000 miles away, we were still in the country, still in the earth.

Even before the judge determined my son to be guilty of those charges, I thought to my self –Lord if my son has to do any time in prison, let it be at the Canton Correctional facility where the team and I preached, prayed, praised and taught the Word of God for seven years together. Surely the brothers incarcerated there would recognize my last name and embrace my son and even protect him from bad influences at that institution.

As a mother of a prisoner you automatically worry about the sanitary conditions of the local jail-whether there is any significant cleaning done at all? Is he allowed to purchase any cleaning supplies? If you had not heard it before now, I am a person with an OCD (obsessive compulsive disorder) –mine just happens to be a compulsive (cleaning) wiper. I spend just as much money on cleaning supplies as I do on make-up. When my boys were young, they knew I was a cleaning fanatic and I've remained to this day. It seems as if I always have a spray bottle of some cleaning solution nearby (home-office-restaurant-especially at a buffet)

I recently read an article involving a young female teenager who was arrested behind a prank at a high school. She, too, was made to sleep on the concrete floor for 3 nights because the jail was out of beds—no beds were available. When my son was placed in jail on the first night after his bench trial, he also had to sleep on the cold jail house floor. What mother would want their child to sleep on a cold concrete jailhouse floor?? No matter what the child did, I guarantee you the overwhelming answer from most of you would be –no, not my child. My heart pained at the thought of how cold he must be—and then I wondered did they give him anything to eat all—and was MY son wearing that easily recognizable orange jumpsuit?

Where are my friends? Being middle-aged, conservative and

Christian, I unfortunately did not open up to anyone in the state of Texas about my family's personal dilemma in Illinois involving the incarceration of my oldest son. This was a private family matter. We had not even been in this state a year, who would I dare open my personal life up to anyway?

I had already turned 51 years old and in this age group-we don't set out to make new friends quickly The ones which we have made already we tend to keep them for life-UNLESS there's a big event like this one. This is the reason why it hurts even more is because I forged several friendships for over 30 years and had been active with several ministries and church affiliations. No one in my immediate religious community sought us out to pray for us and with us, as least none that we were aware of.

Maybe my husband was right, perhaps people didn't know what to say. Perhaps they just prayed and did not feel strong enough to talk about my son's obvious plight. Lastly, perhaps we had been gone from Illinois for nearly 8 months and people just forgot about us. I'm hoping that it was not the latter.

Maybe those of you reading my story have experienced abandonment by friends or to put it mildly, the absence of friends when you need them the most. What do you do when the ones you thought would be there not to 'catch' you but to support you with strong words of encouragement or the bare minimum a message on your answering machine that said-hey we saw the newspaper and we're praying for your family—suddenly fell silent and said and did nothing. What do you do?

I do not want to sound as though there's no grace on my former church family which I felt let me down. There is the small chance that perhaps they don't read the criminal section of the newspaper and maybe they just didn't realize it was my son's name spelled out in the arrest section of the paper.

They heard that I had moved out of state and that there was nothing else which they could do. My husband keeps telling me to lighten up. Forgiveness is wonderful and it promotes inner healing.

At the present, I have not formally united with a local church in Texas. There were so many.

And I want to be sure to unite with the one that best suits me and one that I feel that I can receive the true word of God. I have visited several but have not yet committed at this time.

I am the Mother of a Prisoner and this is my story.

MY FIRST JAIL VISIT

MY HUSBAND AND I had to take turns on visiting my son while he was still alone in Illinois. It was too expensive for both of us to travel each time. The bench trial was attended by my husband and so the all dreaded sentencing day would fall on my side. I had no idea whether I would be allowed to see my son after sentencing so I opted to extend my stay for the entire week. This meant 5 -6 nights of lodging at our favorite, affordable and convenient place, The Red Roof Inn. The staff at the front desk had grown accustomed to seeing one of us at least once maybe twice per year. It's such a small world to the point that one of the front desk staff was a former neighbor of ours who was now all grown up. This meant she was a teenager when we lived on the same street. At the time my kids were both in grade school so she had no knowledge of our son unless of course, she did a name association.

The day of sentencing was to be held on the first Friday in November 2006. Since I always come in town on Sundays, I decided to visit my son prior to the sentencing, on that Monday, which happened to be Halloween. There was nothing tricky about this situation and there was no treat in sight.

On this cold Halloween night in central Illinois, I had dressed as warm as I could in layers because no coats or jackets were allowed. Car keys and wallets had to be checked in at the front security desk. I do recall that the jail visitation hours were very inconvenient. I believe those hours were 6 – 8:30 p.m. on certain evenings during the week and minor children could only visit their parental inmates very early on Saturday mornings.

The waiting room area was very small and only a few visitors at a time were allowed to go back to the actual visitation cubicles. I arrived at the county jail about 5:45 p.m. and it was already dark. I signed in early with hope of getting called back in the first group. Of course I would not be so fortunate.

We had moved from Peoria two years earlier during the fall of 2004. I was on guard because if I recognized someone that I knew in the waiting area, what would I say? I had been an active member of two prison ministry teams for about seven years up until the spring of 2004 and we had visited one local prison plus the work release center, though we had not visited the county jail as a group.

Normally I would bring a book to any appointment which required idle waiting, but not here-I had no one to leave my belongings with when my time to visit would come. Because of the size of the waiting area and not enough seats for the pending visitors if you went out to your car you would lose your seat. From what I recall there were approximately 12-15 seats. It appeared as though there were several people who were there to visit the same individual(s). I know personally that family support is critical to any person who is incarcerated. That Halloween evening when I was at the county jail, ninety percent of the visitors were black. There were also people standing along the walls near the restrooms because all of the seats were taken. My total wait time was about one hour and forty-five minutes before my name was called (actually they call the inmate's name and those visiting that inmate would line up. Only 2 visitors per inmate were allowed at one time. During this wait time I got up and walked around to stretch and relieve my back, someone called out ' Mrs. G' and I was startled of course so I turned to see who it was. Wouldn't you know that this was one of my son's classmates and friends? He was an honorable young man named Braxton, who greeted me with a big hug. He had spent nights at our home when we lived in Illinois while they were still in high school. He had no idea that my son, his friend, was locked up. We chatted for a few moments and he said if he came to Texas he would look us up. I did not feel ashamed like I thought I would, after all he was there to visit a relative also. When the visitation door was opened everyone rushed in to get to an empty cubicle. Next- you had to wait until the guards brought out your inmate. The experience was just like an episode of the TV show 'Law and Order '.

A glass screen separated you from the inmate. The glass was very dirty-full of fingerprints. Because I have an OCD (obsessive compulsive disorder) of wiping down surfaces with disinfectant cleanser, this was very daunting to me-I wanted to clean the glass, the desk top and of course the telephone receiver. What also popped in my mind was an episode of Monk, the OCD detective who used a jail phone with an incarcerated person to get information and he had a napkin or handkerchief to shield himself from germs. When reality sets in and you remember that you haven't seen your child in almost a year, you forget about the germs and everything else –you just want to see your child!

It took the guards a few moments to bring my son out, so I just sat in that chair—looking around at the aforementioned dirty surroundings while remaining anxious to see my son. He's the one who looks most like me. He's tall, dark and handsome and amazingly resembles my deceased father. My son has all of my dad's traits-the way he walks, his height, his easy going spirit but yet he ended up in a place like this. I don't know how this happened. Where did I go wrong as a mother? As they were bringing my son to the visiting cubicle he smiled when he saw me as I managed to hold back the tears. We then had to pick up that dirty phone receiver in order to hear each other. I had told myself that I would not cry in front of him, he felt bad enough already so I was determined to try to be strong for him. He was wearing one of those bright colored jail jumpsuits-he needed a shave and a haircut.

My heart was just crushed. Here I am—sitting in this dingy jail and my son is on the other side of the glass. I have a college degree, I was a licensed minister, former Sunday school teacher and superintendant, professional woman, former Realtor of the Year , have another son who is a young attorney and here I sit looking at my eldest child in a county jail. I mentioned to him that I ran into Braxton in the waiting area and that he was here to visit his brother. I told him that we miss him and that we love him and that I'm still praying that the sentence won't be too hard. My son was facing 30 years- yes thirty years! I asked how he was doing he said alright; but he didn't have a bed he was sleeping on the floor. I said what? Sleeping on the floor? It was the last day in October in Illinois-the temperature that night was in the 40's. Being a type A personality, I almost lost it even in the visiting area of the jail. I could not fathom that my son was on the floor. Being the kind of mother that I am, I had to say something to the security guard on my way out when my visit was over. He did say that he would see what he could do- he couldn't promise me anything. Whenever those words come out of anybody's mouth—my praying intensifies. As a matter of fact I was able to bring him some clean underwear with me to the jail. We also spoke about his son (my grandson) and he also wanted me to start working on his appeal.

At this point my son had already been declared guilty at the bench trial. This visitation meeting is what I refer to as the pre-sentencing visit. The judge's sentence would come in four days and I would be present to hear it firsthand. It was getting late and it came time to say good-bye. The next time that I would see him would be on the morning of the sentence. Since I could not hug my son, all of my OCD issues went out the window and we did place our hands on that dirty glass opposite each other as a sign of love and unity. That is my son in the Peoria County jail. I don't care what he did, he is still my son. Believe it or not, I was able to hold back the tears and I was proud of myself for being able to do that. Now it was time to get my car keys back from the front desk jailer and head back to the hotel. It was getting close to 9:00 p.m. and it was cold in Illinois.

There are several images seared in my mind during this whole chapter of our lives, which I will never forget- one is that of my son in the bright orange jail jumpsuit. It was as if he were a little boy all over again walking towards the seat in the visitation cubicle. He looked helpless and hopeless, but no—Au Contraire—our hope is in Jesus that the judge will render a favorable sentence in my son's case.

Somebody may ask is there such a thing as a favorable sentence? To that I say yes. Anything less than 30 years would be a favorable sentence.

It crushed my heart to see my second born-my oldest living child who is tall and chocolate covered like me, be in this situation. I did not display any embarrassment nor any rage towards this predicament which he brought upon himself. I want to be able to speak up for him and to articulate words for him. That's what mothers do.

During my son's jail stay we did not write letters as he was able to call us collect. This jail stay I hoped would be the end of it all and perhaps he would be given time served and placed on probation which meant he could possible return to Texas with me.

You will see in the chapter entitled 'Sentencing Day" things don't always work out the way you had hoped.

I am the Mother of a Prisoner and this is my story.

SENTENCING DAY

I AROSE EARLY on Thursday, November 6, 2006, for I had spent my last night at the Red Roof Inn in Peoria, Illinois. My stomach was in balls, to say the least, a bundle of nerves. I thanked God for a quiet night's sleep amidst the rumor that the motel office had been robbed that very night and my room was right smack next door to the office.

If I myself had wrestled most of the night I could only imagine the kind of night my son spent at the county jail. The sentencing hearing was scheduled for 9:15 yet I had arrived at the county court house a little before 9:00. Earlier that morning I was up reading scripture, praising God for turning the heart of the judge and for a light sentence.

Now if you've been saved for any length of time as I have and you pray in the spirit regularly as I do, then you recognize the voice of God. The Lord had prepared me for the imminent decision-however some days I would accept it and braced for it; while on other days I wanted to amend what God had already said. One of the questions which I never got a clear understanding was whether or not the judge has the right to rule below the minimum stated sentence for a particular crime. I believe that it varies from state to state and of course if you're a faith filled Christian as I am-the sky is the limit for what I can ask of my Heavenly Father and what I can have.

I did my daily prayer confession that God would indeed turn the heart of the king (in this case the judge) on behalf of my son for me because God's got the heart of the king in His hands and He turns it wherever He wills (Proverbs 21:1). Another confession was

II Chronicles 16:9 –"the eyes of the Lord run to and fro the earth to show himself strong in behalf of them whose heart is perfect toward Him. I was saying hear am I, oh Lord; show yourself strong on my behalf. Hallelujah. Daily confessions are more than just mechanical recitations; they embed the Word of God in your heart and your spirit which prepare you for daily living and battles, whatever the case may be. Your very spiritual foundation is being strengthened by these confessions.

The temperature was quite brisk in central Illinois that morning, approximately 40 degrees. I was glad that I had brought my leather jacket with me from Texas. As mentioned upon arrival at the courthouse, my stomach was tight yet at the same time I wanted to see what the Lord was going to do. I was prepared in my spirit (so I thought) -but as a mother my heart was still grieving over the fate of my son.

Everybody stood when the judge entered the courtroom. After telling us to be seated he told the deputy to get Mr. Godfrey. And then it happened. When I saw my son enter the courtroom in shackles- hands and feet bound-I wanted to scream out No! No! -this is my son! He's not a slave-likened to that which has been depicted in past documentary films. My little grandson was half awake and half asleep in his mother's lap. I don't know if he saw his dad enter the courtroom or not. There was my son, my second-born waddling in the court room in chains. Father, I cannot get that picture out of my mind, it will forever be etched in my heart. I whispered Lord I know that you've got my son in your hands. I now know how Mary felt when she saw her son Jesus in chains, no words were spoken, but her eyes filled with tears like mine. There is one major difference in these two scenarios, if you will, her son was innocent my son was guilty. Please try to understand this comparison. I am making a point here; both sons were prisoners but only one was guilty-mine.

The beautiful thing about our Lord and savior was that He who knew no sin became sin for us that we might be made the righteousness of God in Christ Jesus (II Cor. 5:21). Jesus took away the sins of the world; all we have to do is to receive him, for he will give you salvation. He will also teach you and show you how to live. It is just that simple.

Continuing on in the sentencing hearing, the judge then addressed and instructed my son the reason for the sentence. He stated that it is a method of correction and holding individuals accountable for their actions. Man this judge has excellent bedside manners, if you will, and an answer to prayer. I listened as the judge asked our attorney if he wanted to have a closing statement or anything that would vacate the sentencing itself. Our attorney had indicated to us before the sentencing that the judge had made the wrong decision. Not having gone to law school myself, I could tell that this line of reasoning was not going to carry much weight. Why would any attorney insist time and time again that the judge did not rule correctly? What were we supposed to do about a judge's decision, especially now? Yes, especially now at this time. All along, I had been praying that the Lord would turn the judge's heart in my son's behalf. That's what the scripture said that the Lord can turn the king's (judge's) heart wherever He wills to, and that's what I believe.

Our attorney then indicated to the judge that Mr. Godfrey's mother would like to address the court. Now it was my turn. What I have printed here is my prepared statement of which the judge gave me time to read most of it-not all of it. But here goes. Mind you half way through my speech and the tears came down and I struggled to continue.

"Good morning your Honor. I humbly ask the court to exercise leniency on behalf of my son. He has no prior convictions. The victim, Miss Jones (not her real name) did not seek nor require medical attention after the incident. I ask that the charges be reduced-these two were tussling over a telephone. I have never met Miss Jones, apparently these two had had an on and off relationship for months. My son was not a stranger to her. He should not have knocked in her door. He never hit her. The records show that the blood at the scene was in fact my son's after cutting his hand on a glass picture frame or something. My boys were taught that you don't hit women, anyway. I want him to be an example to my 3 yr old grandson. I plead with you to reduce the felony charges as this may hamper good job prospects. He may not be able to ever vote again. He is only 27 yrs old and is a gifted future Construction Engineer. During this whole ordeal I asked my son did he apologize to Miss Jones, he said "yes mom." I also asked him have you repented of your wrong doing and he said yes and also told him that he will have to apologize to his young son for the time that he will have spent away from him. We now live in Texas after being Peorians for 30 years. This was a bad decision by my son and he realizes it. Anything he broke of hers of course he should pay for it. I simply ask for mercy your honor, my son is not dangerous. From this day forward I believe he will try harder to do the right thing. Thank you for your time your honor."

After I stepped down, the judge began to speak again. The prelude from the judge, if you will, was similar to the course of explaining the crime to a criminal 101. He began by telling my son that in the State of Illinois certain crimes carry certain penalties as well as the intent on the accused at the time of the commission of the act. Even though this young lady may have invited him over to her place, the moment she deliberately chose not to open or even answer the door, that invitation was thereby rescinded and therefore my son had no legitimate right to enter her apartment. Those were the two largest offenses criminal trespass and home invasion. When the judge said that I leaned forward saying "come on now Lord, which direction is he going with this?" I said silently, "Lord you cannot let my son do thirty years; I am waiting for you to turn this judge's heart". My son contends that he thought she was in danger after she had just told him a week or so earlier that she might be pregnant. Because I have never met this young woman, I reserve any feelings to comment about her. The judge went on to say that he has never received as much outpouring of support for any person before, even as late as today-which is the sentencing day-letters asking for leniency for my son. ('Here comes the turning' I said to myself—yes Lord'.) These letters, said the judge, came from all backgrounds, from pastors, homemakers, retirees, church members, and others that he had to forward them to the Clerk of Court to put in my son's file. Letters came from Illinois, Louisiana, Tennessee, and Texas.

The judge went so far to tell my son that he seems like such a nice young man and he really hated to give him any time (of incarceration) at all. The heart turning continues! He went on to say that the legislators have taken that out of his hands and thereby he must impose the minimum term of six years to the Illinois Department of Corrections. He further explained to my son that there may be courses and things that he could take while inside, as well as day for day good behavior, coupled with the time already served in the county jail, he could be out in as little as 3 years.

After that, with my son and attorney already standing, the judge instructed the deputy to take Mr. Godfrey back into custody. There goes my son again in shackles –he looked back as if he too was also relieved that 30 years was off the table. From a distance for one brief moment my son did not look like the man he was, but looked like my tall adolescent boy. Perhaps unaware I did not see him as a young man, I saw him as my little boy being taken off to a place where none of my maternal being ever thought that one of my children would end up. I must remember that in life- things happen and there is no expiration on motherhood; -regardless of the age of the child. Thank you, Lord for a reduced term. Hallelujah! You showed up on my behalf. Now I pray for a minimum or medium secure facility with not too many inmates—one that he would be safe in. That's right. I had already prayed for a fair judge and I believed that this judge was fair and now the Lord will direct my son to the right facility. We don't know if this happens immediately or what. We'll have to wait and see where he will serve out his term. I had already searched out state facilities on the internet. It would be great if he were to land in the Illinois River facility in Canton for this is one where I served as a volunteer for some 7 years and the brethren there would certainly look after my son.

I stated in the beginning that I am not a politician, but this topic of 'imprisonment' which is personal to me, has been and is now a regularly discussed topic within the halls of Congress in some form or fashion for years. The Fair Sentencing Act was sponsored by Senator Dick Durbin(D-Illinois), in October of 2009 and signed into law by President Obama in May 0f 2010. Even though my son's offense did not involve any drugs, and he had already been charged, convicted and served his time while this bill made its way through the Congress, this is still a piece of legislation that is worth mentioning now.

This Act reduced the sentencing disparity between offenses for crack and powder cocaine. Senator Durbin and his co-sponsors, as well as families of the accused and the incarcerated, recognized that individuals faced longer sentences for crack cocaine as compared to powder cocaine. It was the same drug but in two different forms. The Act recognizes that the majority of the people arrested for crack cocaine offenses were African Americans. This was indeed a great bipartisan legislative action which should accomplish what the name implies—makes sentencing fair for all persons.

As a result of this Act, the U.S. Sentencing Commission voted retroactively to apply the new Fair Sentencing Act (FSA) guidelines to persons who were sentenced before the law was enacted. This vote will help ensure that over 12,000 people (majority African Americans) will have the opportunity to get their sentences reviewed and possibly reduced, under certain guidelines. This Act will also bring relief and joy to thousands of other mothers of prisoners within these United States.

When your family is directly affected by an encounter with the Department of Justice and a state's Department of Corrections system(in our case two states were involved) , you began to pay a little more attention to what goes on or what should be going on with our elected congressional officials. What they do is public information as well as how they vote. Please take a moment to see how your senator and representative voted on this and other relevant pieces of legislation.

I am a Mother of a Prisoner and this is my story.

EXAMINING MY FEELINGS

TELLING MY STORY is very important to me but it has also been very difficult to write primarily because I am living this experience every day of my life. As of today's writing, June 2008, my son is within 8 months of being released from the Illinois Department of Corrections. Wait—you said he was sentenced to 6 years and it has only been almost three, what's going on? Well in the state of Illinois, you are given time served for the time he was in the County jail coupled with day for day reduction for good behavior does yield an approximate 3 years of actual prison time. The balance of the inmate's time will be served on parole. This will be covered in the chapter 'Free But Not Free.'

If you are a mother or father whose son or daughter has ended up in the last place that your mind could imagine-a jail or prison, this book is for you. For weeks and months on end I wondered what will people say. Why do I think that I'm any different than anyone else? Besides when the story hits the papers I'm already in another city-another state. I have started a new job where nobody knows me. But guess what? I know me. There are countless dignitaries and celebrities whose loved ones have ended up in prison and they continue on with their lives. Life does not stop because your handsome 6'2" son takes a detour from the life that you've desired for him in order to reap the consequences of his own misguided temperament.

Before I peel off the layers of my own feelings, I want to share with you what my mother felt about what was happening to one of her only two grandchildren(at that time). My mother was in her mid seventies when her grandson, my son, was arrested. She told me that she was disappointed and upset at the same time. Her thoughts immediately went towards his welfare in prison- being able to survive any attacks in prison (she watches a lot of television). She was concerned about little Theo, her great grandson, hoping that he would not forget his dad. As a grandmother and great grandmother, my mom was stern in saying that he (my son) is losing precious time for he could be going on with his life. She was sorry that he got into trouble, but is looking forward to the day when he gets released. My mother said that she only has two grandchildren and that she was definitely going to stand by her grandson. She said "I will send him a money order every month as often as I can." My mother is on a fixed income, but she loves her grandchildren.

My only sibling, my brother, who lives in Shreveport, was shocked when he heard the news. He said there's never been anybody close to our family that had to do time in jail. He was not embarrassed, but was surprised. There was a period of disbelief that he wrestled with. Whenever he sees my son, his nephew's picture, he sees our late father. Remember I mentioned in another chapter that my son is the spitting image of my now deceased dad. My brother went on to say that he feels sorry for my son's son. He also feels that this experience has marred his nephew, but he hopes that my son will learn from this experience and hopefully that it will not scar him for life. My brother asked me whether it was peer pressure that perhaps persuaded him to act in a way that none of us had ever seen. Had he seen someone else go to that extreme and so something like this? No, I responded, it was all him.

Shakespeare said 'to thine own self" be true. You must be true to your own feelings. No one knows you better than you. We cannot lead our lives based solely on our feelings. because feelings do change. Why just the other day I was talking on the phone with my mother, who still lives in Louisiana, when I mentioned to her that I certainly hope that my son, T.J., realizes what he's done. For years, every since he became a father, I had pleaded with him to give his baby's mother at least twenty-five dollars every pay period. At the time, he was still delivering pizza and attending the local community college. He was too stubborn to listen. Now since this interruption in his life occurred, he is not able to send her anything at a time when she needs it most. Her management position was abruptly eliminated during the restructuring of a local retailer which left her to care for their son (my grandson) alone plus her oldest son while barely surviving on unemployment benefits until she can find another job. Now my son is not able to make any financial contribution towards the welfare of his own child. His unwise choices are having a direct affect on the welfare of his son. It is so true that no man is an island and our actions do affect more than just ourselves. If we as a society could just embrace that principle, I believe the world would be a much better place to live.

DENIAL

On rare occasions, I have to deal with being in "DENIAL". It is true that my son had been out of the family home long before this incident happened. He was living on his own, so we did not see him regularly. There were some weeks that we did not see him at all; neither did he call. I said that to say this, once you get used to not seeing a person regularly, you somehow transfer that over to not seeing him for years (now that he's in prison). Then you suddenly realize that you just can't pick up the phone and call him. H-e-l-l-o? You do remember he's incarcerated! You now have to wait for those expensive collect calls from the penal institution. The feeling of denial comes briefly yet it doesn't last long because almost every day on the news or in the newspaper you are reminded that some offense has been committed which has landed some son or daughter in court and on their way to prison. Reality sets back in. Wait a minute. I have a son in prison, too. Let's look at the ultimate form of denial. It's raw and it's personal.

I consider myself a proud professional woman who happens to have one of two sons in confinement. I am proud but I'm not full of pride. Pride could be cancerous if not dealt with early in one's life. Because the Spirit of God lives in me, I try to remain humble but from time to time humility can be a battle. In the case of this episode of my life, it's as if I am this great wonderful Christian sister with good oratorical skills, but now I am forced to down shift my ambitions or deny them because my son is in prison. I am still a mother and yet a lot of my waking energy involves thinking about my son, praying for my son and pondering how will be sustain himself once he gets out. Most mothers would agree that this is an integral trait of our being. You deny yourself for the sake of your child, no matter what their age or the circumstances. You put them first. Internally you say, I can get myself back on track later-let me just focus on getting my child out of jail first and then I'll reboot myself. Trust me, it is not that simple.

SHAME

It has taken me several years to get serious enough to put my feelings on paper so that I could share my story with the world. Thank you for investing in my story by purchasing this book. Even though I am currently working in the social service field, I have met many case managers whose clientele consists 100% of persons who were formerly incarcerated. Many times I listened at how some of them refer to their clients or former inmates in general. I shout inside and think 'you would have a different perspective of your clients if your son went to prison one day'. I dare not say that out loud—not now anyway. The day will come when I will have to let the people whom I've worked with for years know what I've been going through for the past three years. While they all exposed their not so pleasant sentiments of working with formerly incarcerated persons, I harbor my feelings and personal experience in SHAME. I'm quiet on the outside with my head down, but my inside is screaming why you would say that about a person who has been in prison — it's not fair! This was not an undercover sting operation. I was just not ready to share my business. Besides you get a glimpse at how a person really feels about a situation when they comment on something not knowing that your life in currently immersed in the topic at hand.

When will I be ready to tell the world that my son is a prisoner? He's incarcerated-he's what the justice system calls an offender. This in itself is a mouth full to say about your own child. Don't you agree? I shared with one of the case managers today from one of the local mental health agencies that I am writing a book-she snickered at first. Why, I don't know. I probably have almost twenty years of age difference on her and she has the nerve to snicker at me. Perhaps, I thought, snickering is indicative of a form of nervousness for her and discomfort about the subject. Well there's more- she asked what was the book about and that's when my embarrassment, private, none of your business sign went up - I told her proudly that I've got at least two books in me. One is my memoir (which you are reading now) and the second one is also non-fiction about the tragic death of my first born when she was an infant, in the care of a white babysitter.

I was too ashamed to tell her what the title of my book is for concern that she would snicker even more. For years I was a member of two prison ministry groups and we went behind the twice monthly to minister to the inmates. Now, all of sudden my own son is now sitting in a place where they've been sitting for years. What is wrong with me? I can only conclude that I never thought this would happen to me! Even more, this was not supposed to happen to me! Shame will cause you to hang your head low even when you have something instrumental to say which can be very liberating and helpful to others. As you continue this journey with me, you will see what happened to this particular feeling of shame.

ANGER

The feeling of ANGER rises on the inside of me every time I think about what my grandson is missing by not having his dad in his life during the formative years of two and a half through five and half years old. This is a tough time period of any child's life. Yes I am angry at my son for taking this detour at this time in my grandson's life and interrupting our empty nester's lifestyle by having us get ready for him to rejoin my husband and me in our home. I've gotten used to wearing my underwear around the house during these hot Texas summers.

My oldest son had been out of the family home, on his own, for about 6 years until this 3 year detour crept into our lives. It affects us all. Please don't get the impression that I don't love my own son-I love him. He's my oldest living child but he's also the middle child. I've heard it said that the middle child is a brand all to themselves. I love him yet I am ANGRY at what he has put my family through. Is this transparent enough for you? You may be saying to yourself at this point, 'now didn't this author say she's a preacher herself' and she is angry at her incarcerated son? Please recall the purpose of this book is to look at everything pertaining to a mother of a prisoner's life.

Society as a whole shuns an offender-whether consciously or unconsciously. They are clueless how their reaction to the offender's life consequently affects the offender's family-especially the mother's. From time to time I may see something on television involving a job/career and I say to myself 'this is what my son should be doing right now-instead he's in a 6 x 9 prison cell.' My eyes have swelled with water oh so many times since we were blindsided by this event of incarceration.

When an adult child has moved out of your home, out from under your watchful eye, a parent may not know the depths of their child's talents or interests. For example, my son studied Construction Engineering at the local community college and it wasn't until after the house sold and I was cleaning out his old room and discovered a pad of architectural drawings. They were very professional. I don't mean to sound biased but those drawings looked just like those I had seen at the Real Estate developer's office where I last worked in a subdivision before we moved from Peoria. He was really talented. I hate to repeat myself for not wanting to sound biased-but those blue prints were drawn to scale and everything. I was so proud of him and the sad part about it; I did not know that he had even developed such skills. Wow. I made a point to tell him so before we left the state. When I think about that talent and this detour that he took to an

Illinois state prison, yes it makes me ANGRY. My son could have been working in that field right now instead he's locked behind bars with a 6 digit number identifying him-R57102. This Anger soon turned into grief.

GRIEF

GRIEF for a child who is still alive is complicated and very emotional. I am grieving over the part of his life that he was robbed of. Sure he has a temper, but he is far from being a monster. I grieve because at this point in my life, my income is not what it used to be nor what it should be which greatly limits my ability to financially help support my grandson who is the spitting image of his incarcerated dad. I think about how scared my son must have been when reality set in and when he was forced to accept the fact that he was going to jail. On the day of my son's bench trial approximately two years after the offense, he was taken into custody from the courthouse. My husband and I took alternate turns traveling from Texas back and forth to Illinois to show our son as well as the judge that he had family support and that his family was not a bunch of crack heads, thieves or criminals. My son comes from a decent household. How could this be happening to my family? You hang your head in grief and wonder what just happened here. You know the impartation that you poured into his life while he was growing up. You also know that he was disciplined as a child-but look at him-26 years old and headed to prison. That's not supposed to happen to MY son!

In this particular chapter as I examine my feelings, every page on which I share my feelings I am also pouring my insides out to you. With every word, the tears come like waterfalls. What is happening to me? Perhaps I even DECEIVED myself into thinking I'm OK. Maybe I'm not OK? This chapter is very painful. Nobody knows what is going through my psyche and my spirit as I embark to write this chapter at 4:30 a.m. in the month of November 2008. I will pursue and still say "How great God is!" He gave me these feelings and the ability to produce tears.

FEAR

Now before all of the bible readers attack me, I know this feeling of fear has to be dealt with. I do know that God has not given me a spirit of fear-but of love, power and a sound mind. You may ask what am I afraid of. Well for one being fearful of what people will say when it becomes known that Ms. G's son spent time in prison. In case I did not mention it—I am called Ms. G (on my job) here in Texas and was referred by the same name for several years in Peoria. Now this part of fear is minimal because the Lord gave me a healthy dose of self-esteem. I will admit to another component of fear that comes on the scene-which is being fearful that upon his release the expenses of our household will increase to accommodate another adult-the money will be tighter as neither of us is currently making the kind of money that we were in our earlier careers in Illinois. I'm fearful that he may not be able to find a job at all and the two- person household which my husband and I have adjusted to as 'empty nesters' will now increase to the point that we may start to feel the pinch. My son will need everything when he is released-from underwear to outerwear, tennis shoes to dress shoes, toothbrush to hairbrush. He's tall with long arms as well, and most of the clothes in his size are hardly ever on sale.

Someone may suggest that I add 'selfishness' to the list of feelings being examined. Not really, but we're like any other middle aged couple that has gotten the kids out of the home and all of a sudden one is coming back home. Be honest with yourself. I am being transparent because I want you to see and feel what it did to us as a family unit. I said from the onset of this chapter that I will be open with my feelings. I love my son but these feelings are the ones that I have wrestled with many times.

I do have great faith and I yet believe that the Lord will supply all of my needs not according to my income or my husband's income, but according to His riches in glory by Christ Jesus. Yes I know that God has not given me a spirit of fear. Yes I know that the scriptures tell me to cast all my cares on the Lord for He cares for me. I also know that it's not by power nor by might but by the Spirit of God that we will overcome this horrendous situation which has interrupted our lives.

Now for the reader who may not have great faith or who may not necessarily be a believer, I will say "this too will pass". However with Christ in my life, this situation is being endured with more depth and a lot more soul searching. It is really hard to explain, you have just got to trust me on this. While your child (no matter what age) may be incarcerated- you can still make it. Life does go on-it is not easy and I dare say so. This is also where your real family members step up and step in to help cover that child and support him or her emotionally as well as spiritually when the formally incarcerated person re-enters society. This is a different example of it 'taking a village' to do something. The village, per se, won't be raising the former inmate, but showing mercy, love, support and respect that this individual has paid their debt to society and that individual just wants to go on with their life. It is my hope that what ever family or social group that a former inmate is a member of, that the villagers won't keep throwing that offense into the face of that individual.

I'm also fearful that upon his release and he comes to live with us temporarily, he may make the wrong acquaintance(s) in this new city, who may not have his best interest at heart. They may cause him to jeopardize the conditions of his parole and perhaps return back to that Illinois prison and finish out his original 6 year term or longer. This would come real close to killing me especially after all we've done to get him here with us. Please recall from an earlier chapter that my son was facing 30 years for those charges, sentenced to 6 and was released in 3 years. This is the aspect of fear which would try to rob you of your peace. This, I would say, could be the biggest element of fear in a situation like this. It would also try to rob you of your short-lived jubilation of seeing your son or daughter finally walk out of prison only to do a 180 turn and go back through the prison doors ! Now say aloud with me "THIS WILL NOT HAPPEN!" "I MAKE A DECLARATION TODAY-NOT ONLY WILL MY CHILD NOT RETURN

TO PRISON", because of his (her) excellent behavior upon his/her release —"HIS (HER) PAROLE TIME WILL BE REDUCED IN JESUS NAME. AMEN". This elephant of fear is hereby cast down today! Did you know that when you decree a thing, the light will shine on your ways, and it will be established for you? Yes. I got that also from the bible. If you want to read it for yourself, refer to Job 22:28.

GUILT

I believe that I WAS A GOOD MOTHER-with all my heart. The time period which I possibly did lapse from pouring into my son's life was maybe in my early years while in the real estate business. The time when I was an actual co-founder of a small real estate company (no ownership interest though) but all of the ground work foundation was helped being laid by myself.

My former business partner came up with the company name and I was assigned the task of designing the company logo which would be imprinted on our yard signs, business cards, stationery and office window. This would be a magnet for potential clients to distinguish us from the competition. A lot of blood, sweat and tears went into getting someone else's business up and running. My sons were 6 and 7 years old at the time. Real estate was a hard business and we got paid on commission only, but I loved the real estate business.

Perhaps it was during this time when maybe I could have spent more time with my sons and hence I do harbor some feelings of guilt during my children's early years. They never went without real food and clean clothes. I did cook, not like a lot of other young professional mothers. The homework was left for their dad to review. However I made all of the parent teacher conferences and all of their childhood doctor visits. It was back in 1986 when this real estate company was founded called Metro Realty. My son, T.J., was six years old at the time and I was working sometimes 10 and 11 hours a day getting the business set up as well as showing and listing properties. It was a huge undertaking. This start up phase lasted approximately from 1986 -1988 which coincided with grades 1 through 3. Maybe during the hustle and bustle of my early real estate career, too much attention was spent on the business and not enough time for my sons. After the business finally took off; we started getting recognized by customers and also had a couple of other agents join with us. The demand on my time was still high though not as intense as it was during the first 24 months of start-up.

We made it through grade school, middle school and high school. I was keenly aware of who my son was hanging out with, especially when he brought them to our home. How many of you reading this book really know that you can try very hard to pick your son or daughter's friends or associates-but it doesn't always work like that. You cannot blame a parent for trying to pick them-right?

The earlier months of my son's conviction and subsequent incarceration were very hard for me. Saturdays are still hard—no coworkers around, no clients, just you and your thoughts of all that your son is going through and what affect it must be having on my grandson. I have not made any friends in Texas yet, so it's just me. Just the other day on a television program, I saw a tall dark young black man with a hoodie and sweatpants on. I lost it! His physical features were so much like my son. I absolutely lost it! Those tears started coming so fast that I could no longer see the TV set. When my eyes finally cleared they never showed a close-up shot of that young many—but to me—he was still the image of my son.

This chapter could have been an endless one, but I will cover these last two feelings with brevity yet transparency.

EMBARRASSMENT

Unconsciously I was feeding into the same line of would-be bondage by thinking 'what will people think or say about 'me'? Notice that I didn't say what will they think or say about my son-instead I'm concerned about what will they think or say about 'me'. Now that I have put these words on paper-it does sound a bit silly and selfish.

My son is the one who has been separated from his family, his toddler son-who is now in pre-school and I have the audacity to say'

What will people think or say about me?' Lord, please deliver me from this feeling of embarrassment. Only a few paragraphs ago I said that it is a good thing that I don't have self-esteem issues in regards to the feeling of embarrassment. In all of my fifty plus years I can honestly say that I have not been nor do I choose to be a people pleaser.

Admittedly so, it is easy to conquer embarrassment when you live in a city where you are only known by name by just a few people, your immediate neighbors and your coworkers. Sometimes embarrassment takes on a form of denial. At the time of the writing of this particular chapter, we have been residents of the state of Texas for about 4 years. It is very amusing because when we left the state of Illinois I was known by hundreds of people mostly from my days in real estate. I also served on a city advisory commission and on a Non-profit Board of Directors. Since arriving in Texas, I have not gotten personally close to any individuals. Grant it I am a type 'A' overt personality, but when it came to the issue of my incarcerated son-the dialogue was carefully diverted by me with hardly any stuttering. There are the coworkers in my department which I see and communicate with on a daily basis. There are also other persons who work at the agency but I have no direct contact with regularly, and I also have over 200 persons in my client caseload which I see annually throughout the course of a year's time. In conclusion, for Embarrassment to be a major factor in one's feelings, you have to be surrounded by a base of folks who are close enough to you and whose opinions matter and will help fuel that feeling. Good for me, I did not have such a base so consequently I did not harbor this feeling very long, just during perhaps moments of personal reflection when I had to face myself about what was actually happening in our family. During the day at work I could put it on the back burner, but the moment I was alone in my car driving back home, embarrassment was again whispering in my ear.

LOVE

If you are a true mother, this will always be your banner-LOVE. I love my son so much that I would have traded places with him if

EXAMINING MY FEELINGS

I could have. I have a college degree, years of public experience, graduated with honors, so I figured with my background; it would be easier for me to rebound back from being incarcerated than it would him. I know there comes a point in parenthood when you have to allow your children to reap the consequences of their 'not so smart' life choices-we call this 'tough love'. This incident has been a life altering experience to us all. I loved him so much that during his early days of incarceration I began to imprison myself emotionally that is. It is complicated to explain what I mean. I wanted to feel what my son was feeling while he was imprisoned. There would be days that I would absolutely sit in a chair in a daze and run through my mind what I thought my son was going through at every moment of the day. I would cry and tell myself that's my son—how did this happen? Remember I was in prison ministry for 7 years, but our time behind the fence was limited to two hours every visit and then we were escorted back to the gate.

Days on end I would grab one of my family's photo albums from the wall unit and look at his pictures from infancy all the way up to his becoming a father. I would start crying all over again and start mourning about the loss of my son. He is still alive but I mourn that he has been away from us-not leisurely separated but as a punishment. The spirit of God would then come in and comfort me and remind me that my son is still in God's hands.

Loving and supporting a son who is incarcerated is what mothers do. Your prayer life increases because you have to pray that he makes it through his ordeal-you even put your own issues aside to cover him in prayer day by day-hour by hour for you don't know exactly what he's facing on the inside , but you do have an idea. You look up his inmate number and his offense summary sheet on the internet and up pops your child's picture for the whole world to see. At the time of this chapter, my son is in his late twenties but he is still my son! He is still my son. I carried him in my belly for 9 months and when it was time to deliver him, he did not want to come out thereby having to be induced. That is how close we are, he did not want to leave the safety of his mother's womb. Seriously, my labor with him had to be induced. He was the smallest of my three births and put the most weight on my body. What a sense of humor.

I want to say a few things about loving your son (daughter) who is incarcerated but not loving their actions or choices that landed them behind bars. My son still has my DNA, he's tall like me-yet taller and chocolate brown like me and has a great personality, again just like me. Somewhere down the line he took a wrong turn, lost his temper which cost him 3 years of his life. As the late Bernie Mac would say "America", that is still my child and I will always love him. As long as there is breath in my body, I will love my son and support him through this situation and afterwards. Upon his release I will be there for him. When society frowns upon him, I will be there for him. I will be there for him doing what mothers across the nation and across world, do selflessly , telling him that everything will be alright and most of all "mama's here".

If you are reading this and you do have a child (no matter what their age) behind prison walls, they can and will feel your love for them hundreds of miles away. Just remember that they need your support. Keep writing, keep sending pictures, and putting money on the books for them. They made a bad choice, but that is still bone of your bone. Stand up for them, speak up for them and pray constantly for them. They need it now more than ever.

I am the Mother of a Prisoner and this is my story.

ENTRY DENIED

AFTER MY SON'S sentencing, we did not hear from him for about forty-five days, not knowing which department of corrections facility where he would be housed at. When reality set in after the judge's pronouncement, I immediately started praying that the Lord would make a way for my son to do his time at one of the better Illinois state facilities. I had been spending a lot of times on the weekend watching the MSNBC show named "Lockup". I guess you would categorize this as a documentary/ reality show—but the participants don't get a chance to go through make-up, sing, dance, or bow before an audience-this show depicts their lives inside the fence. So being the concerned mother that I am, I did not want my son to end up in a facility where the residents are ruthless, hopeless and a shear disregard for other human lives, which were also doing their time. You probably never heard of a mother praying for a good prison to send her son. I did indeed and the Lord heard my cry. When I found out the name of the facility, I immediately went to the internet. This institution was labeled a minimum security prison and according to the internet— lots of programs were offered to the inmates, including GED classes, some associate degree college courses offered through a local junior college, mechanic programs and others. This particular facility also did work in the quad cities area for the neighboring municipality.

Many years before my son's incarceration, I was an active member of two prison ministry groups represented by three different churches. This is when I found out that my Christian calling was to minister to incarcerated individuals. My tenure with these groups lasted a combined total of seven years, until we moved to Texas. I had received my license to preach under the leadership of one of the local Baptist pastors-- so ministering and teaching was what we did fervently to the prisoners. Finding out later in life that my own son would be sitting in the same seat (different penal institution) as the inmates did, which three times monthly would receive passionate preaching and teaching from a small group of believers, was a rude awakening. We were more than church members; we were believers who took the Word of God and the instructions of our Lord and Savior Jesus Christ seriously. The Lord himself told his disciples, on one occasion, when I was in prison, you visited me not. We were determined not to be guilty of neglecting a charge given to us by our Lord. Of course prison ministry is not for everybody. It doesn't take long to find out who's really committed.

On one of our regular trips out to a facility in Canton, Illinois, I was detained in the waiting area for an hour and a half. This detainment lasted the duration of our chapel services. The institution had not received the results of my TB test. In a facility where the population is extremely tight, the officials are concerned about any type of outbreak. I was one of the unlucky individuals who always tested positive for tuberculosis when the skin test was done, and had to be cleared by way of X-Ray. Because this event was not work related, my insurance did not cover this expense so the cost had to be borne by me personally which I did on one occasion but again the results had not come back so there was no clearance in the system by my name consequently I was not allowed in. It's a good health measure to avoid an outbreak, but for me the Word was burning in my heart that night in particular-yet I was denied entry and could not deliver it. Oh well in life disappointment happens. That was the first denial.

I had a dynamic message ready for the brethren, but I could not get past the guard. We all came in one vehicle, so I had no choice but to wait until the rest of the team completed the chapel service and we drove back to Peoria. That was the longest hour and a half that I have ever experienced. Now let me set the stage; I am in the waiting area of the main guard entry gate. I had my bible, my lesson notes which I was supposed to teach that night—no water, no munchies, just the cold stare from some of the guards. Most of the correctional officers were decent, and then some were power hungry and rude. I always said if they treat the prison ministry team with such disgust, the inmates did not have a chance to be treated with decency-not very often I would imagine. Again, not all of the officers were bitter towards us, but enough were harsh enough for me to recall that treatment we received- six years later in my own personal life. And we were referred to as 'religious volunteers', not visitors. You cannot be a religious volunteer and a visitor. It was either one or the other.

The most memorable chapel service that I can recall with the group(and believe me there were several), was when I was up ministering and as I was looking over the crowd in the chapel, one young fellow, caught my eye, in particular. He looked as if he was not more than sixteen or seventeen years old, and his face looked very familiar. We after every service would hang around as long as the guard would allow us to shake hands and spend just a few moments with the inmates before they were herded back to their dorms. Another young fellow brought this seemingly shy guy to me and said, "Sister Godfrey, this guy said he knows you", and I said "Really? " I asked him what his name was and when I heard his last name, I recognized him. His mother and his other siblings, were tenants of ours years ago—when he really was a child. His tears never stopped falling during the brief moment I had speaking with him. We couldn't hug them—we could only shake hands. I called him son, and told him that everything was going to work out for him—I even told him to try to stay strong and keep coming to these services. I never saw him again. He looked so young until I don't think he had any facial hair at all. He did not look as if he belonged there. You're probably calling me 'soft' right about now. I can be just as hard as the next person, but it was something about looking on the faces of these incarcerated men, that touched me and I started feeling bad for their families. Several of the incarcerated guys at this facility were from Chicago and on some of our chapel nights we would see an old charter bus loaded with visitors. People did what they had to do in order to visit their incarcerated loved ones.

Now fast forward to May 2007 our first trip to visit our son in prison- the Illinois Correctional facility, my husband and I hardly spoke. We always stayed at the Red Roof Inn and the facility was about 1 hour and a half from the motel. We stopped by to see our grandson who is turning four years old this weekend. He has been without his daddy for over 9 months now. My grandson's mother has taken him to visit his dad a few times to keep that bonding strong, especially during my grandson's formative years. At this point, I am not certain where my grandson thinks his daddy is. I will cover that in a later chapter 'What Shall I Tell My Grandson".

It was a bright, sunny, warm, yet breezy day as we traveled West on Interstate 74 towards the prison. The price of gas was 30 cents more per gallon in Illinois compared to Texas. We tried to conserve on gas by not using the air conditioning in the rental car. Neither one us had any idea of what to expect upon our arrival. My husband is not a talker and rarely starts a conversation especially in the vehicle. He and I had discussed a few names and topics that we would not bring up which we felt would upset our son who is already being constrained in a prison facility. During the drive, I was trying to think good thoughts and reminisce about how things used to be. It has been almost 8 months since his sentencing hearing which is the last time that I saw him. That image of my son entering the court room in that black& white striped jail uniform shackled at his hands and on his feet will forever be burned in my mind. We arrived at the main gate entrance of the correctional facility around 12:41p.m. This time was intentional because we wanted him to be able to eat lunch and afterwards we could visit. Actually we were trying to target between two meal times lunch and supper. Upon getting to the main gate we saw two Caucasian officers. We were inside the gate house with another Caucasian visitor and we were told to go back to the 'hole'. (This was a visitor's hub—more like a cage near the parking lot with an intercom system) Being our first trip we didn't know the visitation process. Upon our return to the hub about 30 minutes our names were called and we went back to the gate house. We began filing out the background information and I filled out an additional form showing that I had brought along some books and reading material for my son. All of a sudden the female guard asked me had I visited any other inmates in the State of Illinois. I replied no but I was a Religious Volunteer at the Illinois River facility in Canton, Illinois until 2004. Lo and behold, my name was still showing up as an active volunteer- knowing that I had moved to Texas in the fall of 2004 and here it is 2007 and I'm on the active list. Well wouldn't you know it I was denied clearance and was not allowed to visit my son? After traveling nearly 1000 miles they told me, "No maam, you cannot go in, but your husband can go in." They were quite helpful under the circumstances by giving me the number to the Illinois River Correctional Facility who could clear that up on the spot or the warden could allow it. The female guard did call the warden's number but guess what—no one answered the warden's line. That was the policy and there was nothing that was going to change it –not right then. My husband looked at me with disgust and wanted to know should he go ahead with the visit. Of course you should! I thought to myself that I would just sit there in the air conditioned gate house and wait until my husband finished his visit—WRONG!

They let me sit inside in the cool for about 5 minutes after my husband left to be escorted up for the visit-they then said " Maam, you can't wait in here, you'll have to go back down to the hole and wait or outside or leave. " You have got to be kidding me! (I thought to myself) I knew the 'hole' had no ventilation at all. I started thinking my God- not only will they not let me in to see my son because of a clerical error, but now they're going to make me wait in the hot sun. It was way too warm to sit and wait in the car even though we found a little shade to park underneath. I would have gotten in the rental car and perhaps drove around to find a burger place or something but the area near the prison facility was pretty remote with regards to services. I did not want to get lost while my husband was in the prison visiting our son. I opted to sit on the curb outside the 'hole' and wait.

The temperature at this time was in the upper 70's low 80's perhaps and it was breezy. This was a God sent. I did not feel any bitterness toward those guards, so I used the time to sit on the curb and ponder a lot of things. As of this writing (2013) it would be impossible for me to sit down on anybody's curb due to age, weight and back and knee issues. I was praying inwardly talking to the Lord, thanking Him that my son is in a 'decent' facility to do his time. I looked around at the exterior of that prison. I looked at the large two or three story semi-brownstone gothic looking building with bars on the windows and high fencing (probably 10+ feet high) with large coils of shiny aluminum looking barbed wire at the top at least about 2 ft in height over the iron fencing. The guard escorted my husband and another visitor up a hill so I figured that must be the place for visitation.

I wondered what did it look like inside-was it clean-were the guards decent or had bad nasty attitudes. Then I recalled that I was a faithful member of 2 prison ministry teams. I could not believe it. If you had told me that 3 years after preaching my last sermon to the brothers at the Illinois River Correctional Facility saying goodbye to them, wishing them well because I would be moving to Texas within a few months that I would be sitting on a stoop outside another Illinois Facility waiting to see one of my own sons- I would have said you must be kidding me. But no, it was me. Here I am-my own son locked up in a place where guys who had made bad decisions, guys who had hurt people, guys who had broken the law were kept here. Then I caught myself---my son had broken the law.

Keep in mind this would have been my first time seeing my son since the sentencing Day in November of 2006. We had already seen one Thanksgiving without him, one Christmas without him and within a few weeks of our visit would be his 28th birthday and he will be spending it in a prison. Who would have thought Sister G's son would end up on the inside of a prison facility. This was surreal. In fact I had to pinch myself.

I wanted to say to the Warden, get the Illinois River person on the phone and they can validate that I have not volunteered since 2004—so I am definitely not active as this is 2007. As fate would have it I did not say a word. I remained totally in Christ—I did not say a mumbling word. I prayed in the spirit, hummed some songs and just sat and waited. It was my hope that my son would not have to spend 6 years in this place.

My husband's visit seemed to have taken forever. I chose not to even think about having to use the restroom - but I really needed to go and I was beginning to get really hungry. It was well past lunch time.

I know facilities have to implement certain rules and restrictions but this one seems utterly ridiculous. So what if I was a religious volunteer (which I no longer was) -why couldn't I have still visited an inmate-namely my 'own' son? I had been cleared prior, but nonetheless that's the rule. Because of that I knew that when I got back to the motel, I was going to have to make some calls to the State Department of Corrections and to the Canton facility. Otherwise I would have to wait until tomorrow Tuesday morning to do my leg work. This entry denial happened on a Monday and I was glad we were going to be in town until Friday. But for now, after coming nearly 1000 miles from Texas to see my son in this prison, I was denied entry.

For some reason after leaving the prison with my husband, we were both starved-so we stopped by an Italian restaurant and ordered a foot long sandwich. I had them cut it straight down the middle—half for him and the other half for me. Later that afternoon, I don't know what happened-I got gravely ill. I don't know if I ate that sandwich too fast because we were both famished, or if the traumatic entry denial had disguised itself as stress and attacked my digestive system. Everything in my being was upset-nauseous, queasy you name it –I was feeling it. I was so weak and sick until I was in bed for the rest of the afternoon and all night. The unfortunate part of this sudden sickness was that it continued throughout the next day and I did not make any calls because I was in bed for the entire second day.

I could not believe that I had traveled so far to see my son---couldn't see him and had got bedridden sick. Do you believe that??? Food poisoning you think? No because my husband and I shared the same sandwich cut in half and he was fine. I could not eat anything for that evening or the next day.

My spirit was not going to accept traveling from Texas to Illinois, being denied entry on my first attempt to see him and then getting a stomach virus?? I don't think so. No way was that going to be the end of this trip. It was not acceptable that my husband would be the 'only' family member to see him. I was his mother and I was definitely going to see my son on this trip. My son looks a lot like me and reminds me so much of my own departed father-his granddad.

The entry denial took place on a Monday. Being bed and bathroom ridden Monday afternoon and all night Monday and most of the day on Tuesday, I pulled every strength that I had to at least make some calls on Tuesday. I first called the head of my former prison ministry team, Sister Percy, with hope of getting the name and number of the Religious Volunteer Coordinator of the Canton facility. Sister Percy and I had ministered together on the same team for about 6 of those 7 years. I then found out that the Religious Volunteer Coordinator was off on Tuesdays so this important call would have to wait until Wednesday. Instead of waiting until Wednesday, I decided to call to the State Department of Corrections in Springfield, Illinois besides, all of the coordinators reported to her. I just needed someone with some authority to inform the Warden at my son's facility that I was clear to step inside and visit my son. I was able to reach her and explain my dilemma and how far I had traveled –the whole nine yards. I told her that I was once a religious volunteer but now I need to be cleared for visitation with my own son on the inside of the prison system. Can you imagine how I felt? A seven year faithful volunteer telling the state head of the religious volunteers to make sure that my name is taken 'off' the volunteer list because now I have to visit my own son. According to the Illinois Department of Corrections, you cannot be a volunteer and visitor at the same time.

My last time as an active volunteer was the Spring of 2004 and here it is Spring 2007-three years later and I'm still listed as an active Religious Volunteer in the IDOC system and might I add I now live in Texas. She said that she would change it in her system and to contact my old local chapter to make sure they had deleted my name also. I reached the local volunteer and of course she removed my name and told me the obvious—to contact Springfield. I was already ahead of the game. So two systems had taken me out –let's just hope that the system in East Moline received the internal information from the State system. I asked the State Volunteer Coordinator if she would make a call to the East Moline facility and inform them of my clearance, she said yes. To further push the envelope, I asked her if she wouldn't mind calling me back at my motel room to let me know. You know what- she even did that for me. Wow—it seems as though this mountain is finally coming down. We would be flying out on Saturday back to Texas and today is Wednesday. I decided to give everybody an extra day to update all the computers and return on Thursday to see my son. Friday would be the fall back day, if necessary.

I called my son's facility ahead of our second trip to make sure they had received my clearance from Springfield so as to avoid making that hour and half trip in vain. The response from the guard at the entry gate was very vague so I asked to speak to the Warden's office and I got verbal clearance. Nevertheless I was finally able to get it, yet there was still a question surrounding my being a volunteer or visitor. I knew that before I came back to this place on a return trip I would request something in writing from Springfield which I did when I got home back to Texas. It still took several weeks of calling and leaving messages and an outright motherly plea to get a clearance letter in writing. When I finally received that letter, I made some extra copies because I did not want to go through that again knowing that I planned on having other visits during his 6 year prison sentence. I would make doubly sure that when I returned back to Illinois, that letter would definitely be on my person.

The final time I was denied clearance was a year later on my visitation trip. Yes it happened again. But this time the reason was very different. On this trip I brought my grandson along with me to visit his dad. My name was cleared but because the child's mother had not submitted a letter in advance that I could in fact bring my own grandson along with me to visit my son, his dad in prison, I was again denied entry. Are you kidding me? Yes it really happened. What was I to do? I could not leave my 5 year old grandson on the stoop while I visited, so we just turned the car around headed back to the motel.

I have shared with you three times that I was denied entry to correctional facilities. The first was as a religious volunteer in Canton on the night which I was supposed to preach and twice as a visitor attempting to visit my incarcerated son. There are a lot of great individuals who sit behind prison walls-with one problem, they took the wrong detour. They need our support, our encouragement and our prayers. There are various reasons why an individual would be denied entry to a prison facility, so if you know of someone who has been denied entrance, please tell them not to give up. Remind them that the person on the other side of the fence needs them and wants to see their face. If you've been denied, get up and go again. How dare we faint in the process while our loved ones on the other side of the fence are doing all they can to maintain their sanity and hope. After all, it is a PROCESS.

I am the Mother of a Prisoner and this is my story.

WHAT SHALL I TELL MY GRANDSON?

WHEN AN INDIVIDUAL ends up on the wrong side of the law, it is not a one sided-sphere, especially when there is an absolute family intact left behind. Someone once said that no man is an island (John Donne's Devotions). It is also true when a person goes to prison; the family is left behind to deal with a lot of issues. The issues vary but they include topics as finances (bills), lease agreements (in some cases mortgage payments), children, parents, siblings, spouses, girlfriend, boyfriend and even pets. So if an incarcerated person is reading this book especially this chapter, you can see that your tentacles run pretty deep and it is not just about you and a 6 x 9 cell. People are yet counting on you in the midst of your incarceration. That is why you cannot give up hope of ever returning to the outside world—your family and circle of people who embrace you are counting on 'you'. The reaping part of your newfound predicament, if you will, is being separated 24 hours per day, 7 days per week, and 12 months per year upon years from your family, which is your inner circle. My son has regretted many a days that he would have handled the disagreement with a former love interest in another manner. Life changing moments are all around us and the opportunity exists for us to choose which avenue we want to travel on.

In my son's case, when he was formally sentenced for his infraction, my grandson was about 3 years old-perhaps a bit older. He might have still been wearing training pants at that time. Toddlers at that age can talk and communicate with you. My would-be daughter in law had a very difficult time getting him to use the bathroom. As mothers will attest to it is very hard for a woman to potty-train a boy. My grandson knew his daddy and began to realize that his daddy was no longer around. My son and his girlfriend were living together at the time, so his absence was immediate and obvious to my grandson.

When you are a mother of a prisoner and there are young children involved, how should you converse with the child or children regarding the time period that your son or daughter was (is) away? My situation was not typical. When we were blindsided by this incident, we had already moved almost 1000 miles away from my grandson. I wanted so much to hold my grandson to reassure him that things would be alright and that he would of course see his dad again. But how do you tell a toddler that your daddy is in jail? Babies don't know what jail is. Heck I remember when I was in high school and we took a trip to the county jail—I suppose this was their way of deterring us from a life of crime. I can still see and smell of that place—it was dark—one little tiny window in the hallway and hardly any ventilation. I told myself over forty years ago that this was a place that I did not want to end up at. When you're an adolescent yourself, you don't think about the future of children that you have not conceived yet because you are still a child. This old fashioned method of deterrence did work for me and most of my classmates. Nowadays, jails are not on the list for field trips—they go to museums, theme parks, and the zoo.

You know the bible says that a good man (woman) will leave an inheritance for their children's children and I so much want for my grandson to be proud of this finished product which you are now reading. You will notice that I will continually thank you throughout this book, because not only is this particular subject so dear to me, it is also to hundreds of thousands of other households in this country alone as well as throughout the world.

At the time of this chapter, my grandson is six years old and is

WHAT SHALL I TELL MY GRANDSON?

the spitting image of his father, my son, who is the spitting image of my late father. I declare this day, that the incident which happened to my son will not be repeated in my grandson's life or in the lives of my other grandchildren. I want my grandson to not hang his head in shame when he gets older. I am not sure how he's handling it now, being as though he's in the first grade and remember we're 1000 miles away from him. As a praying mother and praying grandmother-I faithfully lift up my grandson and his mother in prayer, because they too, have been affected my by son's 3 year departure to the state prison. The only way that my grandson will be able to truthfully walk in pride is for my son, his father, to not let this experience hamper his personal goals and aspirations, but use this horrendous experience as a launching pad to catapult him into his God-ordained destiny.

It is my desire to be present or to listen intently as my son handles this delicate topic with my grandson. Besides, my grandson was just a little over two years old when my son was taken into custody. How do you find the words as a father to explain to your son the mistake that you made and assure him that everything is going to be alright? Additionally, it has been very difficult for my son to land employment which is so vital to help support the son that he 'abandoned' for three years. This was the age where my grandson was just beginning to make sentences in his own toddler language.

I want to recall the proclamation that my family signed on Christmas Day 2001, drafted by yours truly in fervent prayer, acknowledging that we are indeed a special family chosen by God and this incident does not in the least bit minimize or change the proclamation that each family member signed on to. When a person does something wrong, it does not change the assignment on his or her life. Remember Jonah, in the bible, had an assignment to preach to the people of Nineveh, whom he did not like. There was a prepared fish (you've seen pictures of the whale) waiting to swallow him up because of his disobedience. But once inside the belly of the beast he cried to God for forgiveness and was delivered out of the fish onto dry ground. Then he took up his assignment with gladness. So yes, even persons in the Bible took detours, came to themselves and still ended up doing what God had assigned them to do. So whether you are in a prison cell or walking around free—God has a purpose for your life. Amen.

Because of my eldest son's unforeseen detour through the criminal justice system, I could not be your usual grandma baking cookies, spoiling him rotten and all the other grandmotherly activities with my first and only grandchild at the time. Aside from the distance between us, Texas and Illinois, I had to pray earnestly and fervently for leniency from the judge and for my son's physical safety going through the various levels of incarceration that he had to go through to end up in the eventual facility where he would serve out his prison time.

I remember on one on my trips back to Illinois, I had asked if I could take my grandson on that one hour and twenty minute journey up to visit his dad. He was so excited. I don't recall mentioning exactly where I was taking him but he knew that I was taking him to see his dad—that good-looking, 6'2" slender build, chocolate brown young man who looks a lot like 'me'.

On our first solo journey together, my grandson was 4 years old so I had to have songs ready, funny stories and rhymes and all sorts of kid stuff in my brain—that I could do and drive at the same time. There was a little nodding by him and if the truth be told, by me too. Don't even try it—if you're reading this book and you're over fifty years old—you cannot do highway driving the way you used to be able to either without getting drowsy. You quickly grab some chewing gum and bottled water and continue your journey. Am I right? On this particular trip, it was in March—which is still winter time in Illinois-meaning that you can't let your windows down for it was still cold. So when my grandson got sleepy, I had to call his name out loud to awaken him. At that age, when he went to sleep and was awaken from his nap—it wasn't always pretty. You'd better be ready for a fighting match on a tiny-tot level. So my goal was to keep him awake for the entire drive. He kept asking "Are we there yet, Grandma? I would answer almost son, not too much farther to see your dad. I must have repeated that seven or eight times during that trip.

He was a real trooper when we finally arrived at the penal institution. I put my purse in the trunk of the rental car, straightened up my grandson's clothing and we got out holding hands and went to the guard's station. You'll never believe what happened next. Now keep in mind it had been close to a year since my grandson had seen his dad and four year olds have to be helped to remember certain things. I did not want him to forget what his dad looked like and me now living in Texas, I did not want him to forget what I looked like. Well the guards checked to make sure that I was on the visiting roster, which was not always the case- already covered in an earlier chapter. They however would not allow me in 'with' my grandson. My grandson was on the visitation list but since I was not my grandson's mother and the fact that I did not have a written statement from the mother allowing me to bring such a young child in there—they said no. They even acknowledged that he was most likely my grandson—for they could see some resemblance but rules are rules and I was not allowed entry with my grandson. Of course I was not going to leave my four year old grandson in the car or at the guard's station to visit my son— so we had to turn around and drive back to Peoria. I put it in as gentle terms as I could to explain to my grandson why he could not go in with me. So if he couldn't go in, neither was I.

Now he had been up there a couple of times before with his mother. Since I was going to be in Peoria for 5 days so you're probably thinking—just get the mother to write a statement and that should suffice. No. Not so quick. My grandson's mother would have had to submit a letter at least 30 days in advance to the warden and wait to get an approval letter from the warden acknowledging that I, the grandmother of her four year old son, did in fact have her permission to bring him to the state prison to visit his dad, my son. Again, rules are rules.

On the way back to the Red Roof Inn where I was staying, we stopped to grab a burger and some milk so that my grandson could eat and finish his nap. I wanted so bad to have that conversation with him-but I had to respect how his mother and my son wanted to handle daddy's prison stay—so he could hopefully understand that it would be a while before Daddy would be able to come home and spend the night with them. What is the gentlest way to explain to a toddler, where daddy is, why he can't come home and why is he there? My grandson's mother has told me on occasions that little Theo cried himself to sleep a lot of nights longing for his dad. My son was able to call them 'collect' the same as he would call us collect. Collect calls from a prison facility are quite expensive, approximately a dollar per minute plus we were being charged a special tax to accommodate these calls on your local phone bills. My grandson would always recognize his daddy's voice. Since my son was not able to see my grandson that often, he was able to speak to him at least twice monthly. I encouraged my son to write to my grandson regularly so that during that 3 year stay in prison, his child would have a physical piece of him to hold on to.

During his 3 year stay at an Illinois facility, my son was able to make some crafts to send to my grandson. On one occasion he made a greeting card and mailed it to Theo. My son and Theo's mother agreed to tell Theo that the judge is the one who will say when his dad could come home. As a matter of fact, my son explained to his son that he was working for the judge and that he could not come home until the judge said so. That explanation should satisfy a four year old until he goes to kindergarten, right?

Kids are cruel; not all of them are- but enough of them will say cruel things. For instance" hey-your dad's a jail bird" or "how many stripes does your daddy have on his uniform" or "hey little jail bird Junior". These are mean phrases that I know kids would say. I've not had a chance to ask little Theo what sort of things have the kids told him or said to him about his dad? Timing is everything. This is the conversation that I will have face to face-not over the phone so that I can see how he's coping emotionally.

2009-

Since my son has now been released-he is living with us here in Texas. He did get a chance to spend the first thirty days after his release with his son and was able to tuck him into bed every night. I have the most precious picture that I took of him holding his son on his lap and both looking at each other. Oh my heart just melts when I look at that picture. That was taken within four hours after he was released and after not having seen his son for almost a full year. Theo's mother did the best she could. Her car died and she unfortunately lost her job so it was doubly hard on her. Everybody pitched in where they could. I wanted so much for her to become my daughter-in-law, and it still may happen. Presently, she is just my grandson's mother whom I have a lot of respect for. Even while my son was incarcerated, I told her that she has to go on with her life and we would not think any less of her-for she is still a young woman.

My son is out of prison now, and paroled here in Texas with us, so the major responsibilities are still on Theo's mother. It is my goal to bring Theo down here for the next school year to take one large responsibility off of her. My son has had a very hard time securing any type of steady employment since his release. I am sure that my son hates his own actions which have changed so many lives around him. But this is what families do—you dig in—put one foot in front of the other and keep moving.

What I want to tell my grandson is that your daddy lost his temper one day and went into his friend's house (I don't want to call this person a former girlfriend—that would confuse matters worse) and messed up this person's apartment. He did not steal anything from this person—he was not using drugs-he did not beat anybody up-he was just mad. So the judge had to punish him by sending away for 3 years and during that 3 year time period your daddy missed you very much and he wants to try to make up that time. I would also tell Theo to hold your head up high—everybody makes mistakes but everyone deserves a second chance. I would also tell him (on a child's level of course) what Jesus said—ye without sin—let him cast the first stone.

My son has stated that he wants to go and finish his associate's degree in Construction Engineering so that he can get a better job to provide for his son. I long for the day when my own son will bring himself to apologize to little Theo for taking 3 years off from his life. Things he missed while he was imprisoned—the potty training ordeal—helping him learn his alphabets—helping him learn to write his name, address and phone number and missed his kindergarten graduation.

What I will say to my grandson is that your dad wants the best for you and wants to make doubly sure that you do not go near the place that he has had to call home for the last three years. Every father wants better for their children-especially their son. The son is the one who carries the family tree and family name. In this particular situation-I refute that adage—'Like Father Like Son'-not so. It is not so number one because my son chose not to follow the example of his father-working always—being there to raise his children and staying clear of jail and the ultimate incarceration—prison. I refute that secondly because I am proclaiming this day that incarceration will not be repeated anywhere within my family tree—nowhere. Incarceration will not occur within my in-laws nor outlaws—nieces nor nephews and not in the lives of my other unborn grandchildren. It stops here and today. I declare it in the name of Jesus. Amen.

For men who are still incarcerated and have been blessed with this book, just remember it is not all about you while you are detained behind the wall. Your family still loves you and wants the best for you even under your current circumstances. They need to hear these words from you that you're sorry for the years/months which you robbed from them and that you will do everything within your power to make that time up. Individuals are sent to prison as a punishment not to be punished while you are there. Being separated from one's family and being denied your freedom is of itself, punishment. My son has confided in me and told me 'Ma, I don't ever want to go back to that place'. I call those 3 years a life changing experience.

What will I say to my grandson? I will tell him to make his dad proud of him to do all that he can do and be all that he can be. At the writing of this chapter my grandson is six years old. Today we celebrated the birthday of Dr. Martin Luther King Jr. It has been 25 years since this was acknowledged as a federal holiday. On today, I watched the six hour movie "King" and tried to put some of Dr. King's accomplishments on the level of a bright six year old boy. I had already been crying during the movie and I wanted very much for him to appreciate what Dr. King stood for and what he did for all people, not just for black people. My grandson has two grandmothers—myself and the other is white. I try to be very delicate when discussing any type of racial matters within the family. Of course when you look at my grandson, you would have no idea that he also has a white grandmother-you see my grandson's mother is bi-racial.

It is very crucial for a son to be with his father as long as and as often as the situation would allow should the two parents not be married to each other.

A father's presence and influence is priceless and will have an everlasting impression on how that child (boy or girl) advances through life or not.

I am the Mother of a Prisoner and this is my story.

MY SON IS NOT A STATISTIC

THIS CHAPTER REFLECTS on a personal declaration that I made many years ago when my boys were yet adolescents. I never spoke it out loud but I knew within myself because I knew my internal make-up was that of an achiever-a difference maker, a woman who could articulate her position and feelings at anytime to anybody.

My own teenage years came on the heels of the "I'm Black and I'm Proud" movement if you will-because I am black and I was proud and still am. One of my high school teachers added a phrase to that renowned song-she added yes, you're black and you're poor. We all laughed and left it there. Now that I am what you may call a middle-aged Christian woman, I so recognize the power of words. I might have been poor, but I hearkened within myself as a youth, that I was not going to stay poor.

When I was in junior high school, I cannot recall the subject matter, but we took an unusual field trip to the county jail. It is amazing how your life takes certain paths and you're not sure how the pieces will fit together, but as you age you begin to reflect backwards. I can remember that the jail was a dark, dingy, odorous place with poor ventilation and as a young person I determined that I 'never' wanted to end up in that place. Back then I remember people were all crowded in only one or two cells. I now know that is referred to as the 'holding cell'. I am trying to be as accurate as possible, because glancing into this part of my past occurred well over forty years ago.

As the woman in the bible said to "herself" if I could just touch the hem of his garment then I will be made whole. Little did I know I was making a proclamation-by "saying to myself" that the jailhouse is one place that I never want to end up in. Fast forwarding until now, I have learned that it is not what people say about you or what they say to you; it is what you say to yourself and about yourself. Chew on that little nugget. Amen.

My hometown, in Northwestern Louisiana, was a racially segregated small town and was the parish seat. In Louisiana, counties are referred to as parishes. One of my classmate's father was a decorated officer in the Sherriff's department-which is probably how we were afforded the privilege of visiting this seemingly God forsaken place. They probably had hopes of discouraging our future actions and conduct from having us return to that jail or any jail later in life. Years later there is a nationwide incentive in some states called "Scared Straight" which is a hands on approach to deterring troubled youths from doing just that. Our little excursion was a small town precursor of the "Scared Straight" program on a much smaller scale however. The difference is that none of the students on our field trip were troublemakers, compared to the Scared Straight program targets those who are already displaying signals of perhaps landing in serious trouble and ultimately in jail. That message got through to me at the age of thirteen. Who would have thought that forty years later I would have a son who ended up in a place just like this, in another state? That thought never entered my mind. Surprise, life happens.

My son is not a statistic because he comes from a complete household; a father, mother, one brother, family dog, his own bedroom, two-car garage, fenced yard, the all American family. I point this out because nearly every report pertaining to incarceration mentions the purported suggestion that nearly all inmates come from a broken home which they say contributed to a child growing up without parental guidance and ending up in prison. My son is not a statistic because in contrast to most articles written and various professionals' summation that most inmates do not have a GED, but conclude that the average state prisoner has a 10th grade education and about 70% have not completed high school. My son received his high school diploma on time in 1991. He was the odd man on the inside and he tells me that his cellies (cellmates) repeatedly told him that he should not be in there-(somebody screwed up they say). This made my son feel real special to know that he did not fit the mode for an average inmate-based on the inmate standards of perception and appeal. The other inmates could tell that my son was a fish out of water. My son was incarcerated in 2006 and as of December 31, 2006 the Department of Justice reported that there were 2,258,983 persons incarcerated in prisons (both federal and state) as well as in local jails. That number represented a 2.9% increase from year ending 2005. What this means is that out of every 100,000 American residents, 501 were sentenced to prison during the year which my own son was incarcerated. At the end of 2013 there were 1.57 million persons incarcerated in the state and federal prisons and 731,200 in the local jails within the United States according to the Bureau of Justice Statistics which combined totals approximately 2,301,200 total persons incarcerated in this country at the end of 2013.

If we just take a peek at the racial make-up of these statistics, the numbers are quite disturbing. At year end 2006 (the year of my son's incarceration) the Bureau of Justice Statistics bulletin reports that there were 3,042 black males sentenced to prison per 100,000 black males in the United States. Compare this number to 1,261 Hispanic males sentenced per 100,000 Hispanic males while only 487 white males sentenced per every 100,000 white males. Now it is apparent to any person who can decipher numbers that using the same baseline of 100,000 resident males per ethnic category, the number of incarcerated minorities are leading the charge with respect to being imprisoned. I am not a statistician, but I am a realist. For blacks to represent approximately 13% of the U.S. population yet represent the largest block of incarcerated people, means something is terribly wrong. This blatant disparity recently was commented upon by then

Attorney General Eric Holder in August of 2013 where he stated the people of color face stiffer penalties when they're in the criminal justice system their white peers for the same crime. He went on to say that black male offenders receive sentences that are 200% longer than whites for similar crimes.

"This is not just unacceptable, it is shameful" stated Mr. Holder. I am not advocating opening the prison doors and releasing a stated number of minority prisoners to lessen the inequitable percentages. This disparity should not exist at all, if 'Lady Justice' was as really blind as the statute depicts. In a lot of cases, it really makes you wonder. When two people are accused of the same offense and receive a 200% disparity in the sentence rendered-something has gone terribly wrong and needs to be fixed. Some things should be apparent based on the sheer number of populous within the ethnic backgrounds. Are the judges rendering such sentences declaring that one group of individuals in this country is less inclined to commit certain crimes just because of ethnicity and let's not forget economic status? God forbid. The Attorney General also proposed ending mandatory minimum sentences for some non violent drug offenders. Mandatory minimum sentencing has contributed to a lot of prisons and jails being vastly overcrowded. The criminal justice system itself has practically become criminal when you parallel the same crime = different time levied.

The United States of America represents only 5% of the world's population and yet we represent 25% of the world's incarcerated population. In essence, the United States is known as the world's jailer. Is this something that we should be proud of? I think not! Since 2002, we have continually had the highest incarceration rate in the world according to the Population Reference Bureau. China ranks second and Russia third.

My son's situation caused many of the older inmates at his facility to also question him by saying: Dude, why are you up here? They had accepted punishment for their crimes, but even they could not fathom why knocking in your girlfriend's door without a weapon, without putting a finger on her, without burning down her place, without touching her children, would land you up here with murderers, gangsters, drug dealers, child molesters and the like. That was nice for them to be so comparatively colorful towards my son, however the State of Illinois declared otherwise.

Since we have been going through this ordeal, I have personally noticed that the same offenses in different states carry different levels of punishment. I will say that prior to this event of incarceration landing at our home, I really had not paid as much attention to the disposition of sentences at all, let alone the disparities. This was definitely an eye opener. There have been instances particularly in southern states where people kill other people, dismember their bodies, hide the evidence and claimed to have done this out of fear. Such individuals were punished by being given a smack on the wrist, pleaded fearing for their lives and in some cases probation-meaning no jail time. Does anyone other than me find something wrong with this? Well just in December of 2013, a teenager who had been drinking In North Texas was given probation for a DWI charge which killed 4 people. His defense team claimed that he was suffering from ' affluenza ', a case where his family is so wealthy that as a child nobody disciplined him –and there were never any consequences for his behavior, so he was just lost while raising himself. OMG, the judge bought it and the rest is history. Can you imagine how the surviving family members left feeling when that verdict was read? This impact was felt across the nation and people are still up in arms about this verdict. In fairness to the family of the accused, this is just one of many cases where the justice system, I feel, was made a mockery of and the lives lost were deemed insignificant as a result of the judge's ruling. Was the judge's hands tied because of state statute or did the judge decide not to use her own discretion? We may never know the answer to this and many other tragic, yet baffling judicial rulings.

Even though my son has now been released, while we were waiting for his sentencing day, I never asked the individuals to write requesting a dismissal- only for leniency. We asked for leniency for I knew in my heart, as I stated in an earlier chapter, that my son would have to learn the hard way that his actions, which were nothing compared to the previously mentioned teenager's case, had the ultimate consequence-time in prison and a felony record. This justice system must be fixed. Improprieties in some judges' decisions may potentially send subliminal messages to the world and crash the entire judicial system and certainly not for the better. This book is not meant to incite, only to give a glimpse of what is happening in our world in regards to imprisonment.

As a mother of a former prisoner, I still feel that my son's penalty was severe. He and this young lady were not strangers because they had been dating for a while. She had invited him over that night but he was late as usual getting there and due to his lateness, she decided that she did not want to be bothered, with him anyway. So she chose not to respond to the bell ringing, door knocking or his phone calls. I do admit what my son should have done at that time when she didn't open the door, was to leave the premises. They had apparently spent quality time together previous nights so in his mind, something had to have gone wrong. So he panicked, without thinking, knocked in her front door and the rest is history.

Because of my son's failure to pause, think and leave, he has a felony on his record. I never realized the severity of having a felony background. It sounds serious, but not until it hits your front door do you realize the intense magnitude of this label. During the writing of this chapter, my son is out of prison but yet on parole for three years. I am hoping that if his good behavior continues, his parole time will be reduced just like his original prison sentence. I always expect what some say can't or won't happen.

Yet I know in whom I believe and with God, all things are still possible. I am expecting that my son will get off parole within the next 12-15 months and rejoin his son in Illinois.

The rate of recidivism for parolees is quite high especially if they have no family support system and no employment opportunities and drug abuse issues almost quantify the rate which a parolee returns back inside the prison walls. My son, the parolee, does not fit any of these categories for which I'm grateful and he will not be one to return to prison. Right now we're all he has. This unfortunate incident of incarceration, I do believe, has made us stronger as a family. In this chapter he has been out of prison for 1 year and 1 month.

In 2008 alone (the year preceding my son's release) there were over 730,000 individuals released from prisons which is an 8% increase of the persons released unconditionally. There is a definite need for re-entry resources for the state and local service providers. My son was released with these conditions: reporting regularly to his Parole Officer (PO), random UA (urine analysis) tests, anger management classes and drug abuse classes and actively seek employment. I asked him why they are having you take the drug abuse classes. He said he didn't know- it's a package deal and it is a condition of my parole. Financially speaking he also has monthly parole fees to pay.

My son is not a statistic. He was not supposed to end up in prison. The only category which I will concur that he paralleled was the 18 – 34 year old group of black males which have a high percentage chance of being incarcerated during their lifetime. His dad, my husband, was indeed a present force in the home unlike that which the statisticians forecast and conclude. I soon found out that as a Texas parolee-you do your time on paper—paroles are not reduced. Wait a minute, the Texas Parole Division is overseeing my son for the state of Illinois. In Illinois, the parole period can be reduced. I know it sounds as if I want my son to have the best of both worlds. Sure, wouldn't you? Why could he not adhere to the Texas Parole Division while living down here with us, but exercise the Illinois parole department discretion based on good behavior with possible early release and return to Illinois to be with his son? I have no problems sending a letter to his parole officer, but it will probably be more effective coming from my son. Sometimes I still forget that he is a grown man and I want him to make his own decisions. He has told me that sometimes I do strong arm him to do things (such as writing and calling) which are not who he is. I must learn to let my son be himself, and to do what he feels will be helpful in his situation.

I will always remain close enough to whisper a suggestion " why don't you do this, why don't you call over here"—but in the end, he must exercise certain options himself.

The reason which I wanted to include this chapter is to hopefully dispel stereotypes about incarcerated individuals, their socio-economic backgrounds and their families left behind.

I am the Mother of a Prisoner and this is my story.

RELEASE DAY

WE LEFT TEXAS early one Saturday morning with plans on being in Illinois by night fall. It generally takes us an hour or so longer due to my needing to stop more frequently to walk around, stretch my legs and straighten my back. I try to make a run to the chiropractor before long trips and afterwards especially. However for this trip, time did not allow. My chiropractor suggests that I stop every 2-3 hours for stretching otherwise it would be very difficult for me to walk once I reach my destination. My son was scheduled to be released from the Illinois state prison on Monday, February 9, 2009 at 8:00 a.m. He served three years for the charges that he was found guilty of. The balance of the other three years would be served on parole, as my clients have educated me to the reference of being "on paper".

It was a long quiet drive from North Texas through Oklahoma, up through Missouri and on into Illinois. The last time we actually drove to the state of Illinois was when we pulled up stakes and departed the Midwest in October 2004 and moved to the great state of Texas. All other travels back and forth for the bench trial, sentencing, visitations and appeal hearings were done by airplane. As I mentioned only on one plane trip both my husband and I traveled together for our first visit to our son, all others we alternated turns due to the expense of flying, hotel costs and rental car expenses.

Even though it was still winter time, we had good travel conditions over the highway which was an answer to prayer. No snow or ice to contend with. Praise the Lord. I'll never forget one return travel from our hometown state of Louisiana as we were headed back home to Illinois; we experienced our first white out coming through Missouri headed towards St. Louis. My husband was behind the wheel and it was as if someone placed a white sheet over the front windshield and we could see absolutely nothing. We were familiar with that stretch of Interstate 55—we couldn't stop even though I was screaming for him to stop. He hollered and told me to shut up and reminded me that if we stopped one of those semis would rear end us and run us over; so it was better if we just kept going and hoping that no other cars would stop or we would rear end them. I prayed continually and pleaded the blood of Jesus over us as we continued—this seemed to last forever but truthfully it was only about 10 minutes on a straight stretch of highway driving blindly and all we had to do was to keep driving and we eventually drove through that white out. I never want to repeat a driving experience like that again. I took time to thank the Lord for good traveling weather on today.

Because my husband and I are 'empty nesters', we actually spoke very little during this fifteen hour drive. I was wondering in my mind had he(my son) gotten taller. Then I reminded myself, he was a grown man when he went in, his height of 6'2" was already established. I also wondered had he picked up any weight since the last time I saw him has been close to a year ago.

I actually dreaded the long drive because of my back issues, but this trip was one which I endured proudly because our son was coming home. Since I've been in my fifties I do not like to drive at night. Sometimes, the other headlights are blinding and sometimes I cannot see the dividing lines on the dark pavement. My husband and I rotated driving turns along the way. As we approached southern Missouri the nightfall was bearing down on us. It would be pitch black before we reached Peoria. We forgot that during the winter time, it's dark around 5:30. My husband wanted to push and drive all the way through which meant we would arrive in Peoria after 10:00 p.m. I knew that I would not be able to relieve my husband driving at night and he knew it. I had another reason for not wanting to drive through. There was a special movie first time being seen on television which was to air @ 8:00 that night. It was the Ben Carson story, "Gifted Hands", which I definitely wanted to see. I had claimed Dr. Carson as my mentor, even though I never met him. I had purchased and read all of his books with the exception of his latest one which was coming out this year, about America.

This movie would be a shot in the arm for my intellect and my soul under such circumstances which we were traveling to Illinois. It would remind me that even though his obstacles were different than the ones which my son would be facing-I wanted to embrace the life changing nuggets which I was sure to see in tonight's movie. Besides what's the harm, we had room reservations anyway for tomorrow Sunday morning, if we arrived tonight; there was no guarantee that the hotel would have a room for us. I didn't have to work hard to dissuade my husband from driving through the night, he concurred and we pulled over, got something to eat and stayed over south of St. Louis. We checked into our room just before 8:00 that evening in time to see the movie. Chalk one up for me, I got my way!

On Sunday morning, we were within four hours of Peoria. We arose, got breakfast, got gasoline and hit Interstate 55 North toward Peoria. We arrived in Peoria around noon with our clean room waiting for us. We checked in, freshened up and relaxed before dining for supper. We called and left word with our grandson's mother that we were in town and we would see them some time tomorrow with our son. Neither one of us could sleep that night. Our son was due to be released at 8:00 in the morning. The prison facility was about an hour and a half from where we were staying. You have to understand the butterflies swarming in my stomach, the jubilation we were feeling, the smiles and the tears of joy that I was shedding that night. Thank you Lord this day was finally getting here. We get to take him back with us. He had requested to spend parole in Texas with us. I had communicated back and forth with Texas Parole division and with the Illinois state parole division—so everything was set. I had started making phone calls and faxing information weeks prior, because I know how things happen. I was feeling assured that everything was covered.

When we picked him up, he would be staying at the Red Roof Inn with us-the officials had that address and phone number. So tomorrow would be Monday and we plan on staying all week, so he could bond with his son a few days before driving back to Texas with us.

We arrived at the East Moline Correctional Facility at 7:45 on that joyous Monday morning. My husband and I were anxious and we both had cameras. We were familiar with the routine of going to the guard house after parking the truck. A female guard came to meet us before we arrived at the guard house-what was up? She politely told us that we could not take pictures of the prison and that he was not ready to be released just yet. What? She said not to worry, we should go to a nearby eatery and get some coffee and breakfast and to come back with half an hour. She stated that the inmates were being "counted" and it should not be too much longer.

I took a breath and exhaled. We said alright, we'll be back. Prisons as buildings don't really have character, so if I had to describe the exterior of this particular penal institution, I would call it Gothic-like or Victorian style architecture. The bricks and stone were blonde colored and surrounded by miles of 10-12 ft high fencing with an additional 2 feet of coiled spiked wiring on top. I am not sure if that coiled wiring on top was hot wiring or not. This was a Medium Security prison.

The main gate resembled a small building similar to what you would see at a Rest Area while traveling. The flag pole outside the building had 3 flags flying: the United States flag, State of Illinois flag and the POW (prisoner of war) flag. I made a point to pay special attention to as many details that I could (since we could not take pictures) because I was already in the process of writing this book as I was also living this experience simultaneously. For the past 3 years I have had notebooks upon notebooks, jotting down points, questions, experiences and the like as we journeyed through this prison ordeal.

We went to a local McDonalds and grabbed a light breakfast and we brought an extra breakfast sandwich and juice for our son. We did not want to be late returning which might have given them cause to delay his release even the more. We have come too far, and we were not leaving without our son. I felt a ' mama bear' surge rise up on the inside. It has been nearly a year since I last saw my son. I wonder has he lost weight. The last time I saw my son he had buffed up because he had been working out with weights and playing basketball.

It was very cold on the February 9th morning in Illinois, 2009, so we waited in my husband's F 150 truck with the heat on until we saw him walking down the hill toward the guard gate. There he comes. There comes my oldest son, my second born, tall, dark and handsome walking carrying a small bag full of his belongings (books and leftover toiletries). He had on light gray hooded sweatshirt, gray sweat pants and white tennis shoes. This departure attire was compliments of the State of Illinois. I was so glad I had remembered to bring him a jacket-for it was cold in Illinois. I also had packed him changes of clothing and fresh underwear since we would be in town a few days. He grinned as he walked toward us, I didn't run to meet him, but I walked fast to greet him, we hugged and I said Hey, son and he replied hey mom—let's go! He greeted his dad—we snapped pictures –one while he was walking towards us with his only remaining belongings grinning toward us. In his eyes I could see he was glad to be leaving that place. I thanked the Lord over and over again that my son was free again. We talked in the truck all the way back to the hotel. My son said he had been up ever since 4:30 a.m. Processing an inmate for release does take time. He recited his inmate number R57102 for the last time and we left the East Moline Correctional Center headed back to Peoria. He responded to all my questions but he did not initiate much dialogue. The look in his eyes and the pep in his step as he approached the truck indicated that he was so ready to go home, leave this place behind and be with his son. Getting released is only the beginning of the continuation of his adult life on the outside of the fence-a road that none of us has traveled before under these circumstances.

RELEASE DAY

The Red Roof Inn is the place we always stay when we travel back to Peoria. It's centrally located, just off the interstate; nearby restaurants and not too far from our grandson. We wanted our son to have a chance to relax a bit and get some lunch before having to report to the parole office in town. He would soon be fitted with a monitoring device-I call it the leg bracelet. There were quite a few business issues for my son which had to be taken care of while we were in town; such as getting a new driver's license, new social security card and some actual parole papers. We did not know at the time that the parole division had not approved the Red Roof Inn for my son to spend the balance of this trip at; so consequently he would have to stay at his son's mother's home-which had already been cleared by the parole division. At least he would be able to spend more time with his son and we would come by during the day and take him to handle his affairs. My grandson was in the first grade at this time. One of my son's friends had my cell number and of course called for my son. They surprised my grandson at school-who was elated to see his dad after such a long time apart. What a reunion.

As I mentioned the plan was to spend those remainder 3 days in Peoria and hit the road on Friday back to Texas. Sometime during this period we find out that my son had not been cleared to leave the state of Illinois. Excuse me—this was the reason which we drove nearly 1000 miles to get him and bring him back to our new home in Texas. Before I left Texas I had made numerous calls between both the Illinois Department of Corrections and the Texas Department of Corrections and I was sure everything had been cleared. Not so! My son was going to have to remain in Illinois until the two correction offices agreed with each other's terms. After everything which my son (even though a grown man) had been through, I did not want to leave him back in Illinois, away from my watchful eye. I knew that he would be safe in 'my care'.

But bureaucracy had its way and there was no fighting it. It would be unforgiveable for some other incident to happen after we returned to Texas, which could have easily caused my son to be returned to the East Moline facility. I could not fathom that-so again I was in deep prayer daily that the Lord would keep him safe and eventually he would be allowed to join us. The Lord had already answered my prayer by releasing him early unharmed and now he would be on the 'outside' yet under the Illinois Department of Corrections supervision by way of a parole officer.

The concern for me was that he and my grandson's mother are no longer together, and she has a boyfriend. I cringed when I thought about what could happen if the boyfriend came over and saw my son and a situation could have easily occurred between the two men. I knew my son would not initiate a fight after just leaving prison-but the boyfriend might intentionally try to provoke him enough to incite a parole violation. That would have been awful. Nothing of the sort happened. No troubles at all during those 30 days away from mother's reach. He received his paperwork from Illinois and an acceptable arrangement was worked out with the Texas Department of Corrections to oversee the balance of my son's parole. Our home in Texas had already been cleared as his parole residence.

My son was given 2 days to travel to Texas alone by Greyhound bus and no ankle monitor. He was given a specific time to meet with his Texas parole officer. I picked him up at the Greyhound station in Dallas and had to take him directly to his new parole officer in Fort Worth. There he was fitted with a new ankle monitor and was given a class schedule which he would have to adhere to.

Well, he was released, and this was the beginning of the three years required to be on parole, under supervision. The parole experience and the effect which it had on the both of us is covered in the chapter 'Free but not Free'.

I am the Mother of a Prisoner and this is my story.

FREE BUT NOT FREE

IT HAS BEEN approximately 45 days since my son was released from prison and is officially "on paper"-meaning on parole. He has done his time for that offense but the state still has 'papers' on my son. Did you just hear what I said? The state has papers on my son. Quick history recall-remember when the slaves were initially freed- they were not able to travel (even on the everyday streets) without having papers to prove their freedom and had many limitations upon their every move. It makes you feel as though your child is an indentured servant.

He was no longer in a 7 x 9 cell; he has his own bedroom, own bath and run of the whole house-including the refrigerator. This I know he missed while he was incarcerated. It has been so long since my son has eaten in our family dining room—Wait—he's never seen this house! We purchased this home while he was in prison, so the first time he saw our home was when he arrived in Texas after being released. I forgot what a healthy appetite he had. He has seconds on everything—man can he eat. It does a mother good to see her son enjoy the food she's prepared for him. No more prison food. I am a fairly decent cook, but since both of my sons have been out of the house, I had cut back on cooking. News flash—the pots and pans are rolling again. There is no mother, no matter how old her son is, that won't find something in the kitchen to make a meal out of for her prodigal son who is now home.

This will be an adjustment for us all. No longer can I walk around the house in my underwear no matter how hot the Texas heat gets.

Did I mention that at the time of this writing I'm dealing with hot flashes? I cannot shed as many clothes as I did before my son rejoined our household.

One requirement of my son's parole is to submit to a home confinement device commonly known as an ankle monitor. Four days out of the week he would have limited access out of the house until 8:30 p.m. and the other 3 days of the week his feet could not touch the grass outside. The time period for this restriction was left to the discretion of his Texas parole officer. I forgot to mention that even though the offense happened in the state of Illinois, it almost took an act of Congress for my son to be approved to spend his parole in the state of Texas. As his mother, I did not want my son to return to the same state which had incarcerated him and expect the parole process to be without incident, while I was down in Texas. Oh no—there was no way I could rest if this had not been approved.

Mama Bear took the reins, prayed and corresponded with the Department of Corrections in both states to see what needed to be done for this to happen. I did not want to wait until the last minute. I believe that I started the inquiry process 90 days before his targeted release date. Of course my son was also a willing participant in this process. I knew within myself that if I had him here with me, there would be no question that he would be in good hands and I, Mama Bear, would watch out for him. Mind you that the Lord was the ultimate petition grantor in this tedious process, by intervening in the hearts of those who were responsible for reviewing my request in both states. Texas would actually be overseeing the parole time of an Illinois felon. It got real complicated, but thanks to God, the request for Texas to administer the parole of my son was granted and agreed upon by both state Departments of Corrections. The state of Texas could have taken the position that "we have our hands full with our own parolees and you're asking that we take on one of yours"—"Seriously???" But they did not take that position and my whole family was grateful for that.

While wearing the ankle monitor, there was no such thing as me

FREE BUT NOT FREE

pulling up in the attached garage and asking my son to come get the groceries out of the car while on an 'off' day no matter how bad my sciatica and lower back were hurting. He could not even go in the garage. The reason we know is that we tested the system one 'off 'day and the alarm did sound. It startled both of us. Going to the mall or boating at the lake was impossible when that time period fell on a limited movement day or an 'off' day. I understand that persons who have committed offenses in society must pay their debt to society and must gradually be re-integrated into society. I get that. Even as a mother there is nothing I could do or say to make the process of re-integration any less painful than it was. I was prepared to coach my son when he needed coaching to complete job applications, which I downloaded for him and to help him prepare his resume'. I also rode his back until he completed several applications.

Tough love was difficult to give him when I know that he has just gone through the most difficult 3 years of his life, while at the same time I knew it was for his good. Too much precious time had been wasted (in prison) and I knew that he would be up against recent college graduates in the job market as well as folks who had lost their job due to companies downsizing. My goal was to push him ahead of the line, knowing well that the felony offense was a strike against him. As I have said before and will probably repeat in another chapter— in life THINGS HAPPEN. You cannot remain idle-you must "keep moving"—even with an 'F' on your record. You're free but you're not free.

My son refers to being on parole as another level of being in custody. You are not free until you are totally 'off paper' completely with your parole or probation. In addition to the ankle monitor as a condition of his parole, he was also required to attend anger management and drug treatment classes. I can see where the anger management class would be of help, but my son did not use drugs. He would also have to see his parole officer monthly, allow monthly home visits and submit to monthly drug tests. To further lend a hand to the inconvenience, his parole officer was located in Fort Worth and we live in Arlington. The city of Arlington has no real means of public transportation and with the 2 cars in the family being used by my husband and me to get back and forth to work, my son had to walk a mile from our home to several establishments for job prospects. Again Mama Bear pushed him to knock on as many of those establishment doors for employment during the time periods that the ankle monitor would allow. I was so insistent to the point where my son said "Ma, they won't hire me for retail with a Felony background!" I would not accept that, but I backed off and continued to pray that the Lord would open the door of a business who would give him a chance even with that background.

My question is how will an ex-felon feed his son (or in other cases his family) if no company will give him a chance to work? With so many doors closing in his face, my son's frustration was mounting. You mean you can't even work at a burger joint? My son has a high school diploma, some prior work experience and was within 12 credit hours from getting an Associate's Degree and still has had a hard time getting employment. I spoke to an employee at one of the nearby grocery stores and inquired if a person with a felony had a chance of getting hired there—she said sure. But because he bagged groceries while in high school, I could see it in his face that he felt embarrassed that a grown man would have to bag groceries. I tried to enlarge his vision as I searched the internet for that particular grocery store to see what benefits are available for their employees in regards to stock options, etc. My suggestion to him was to start in one area and gradually work in the other departments so that you could be proficient in all departments, with the understanding that you would probably never be a cashier. What's wrong with that? I thought nothing's wrong, but unfortunately he chose not to apply at the grocery store. The old adage is true-you can lead a horse to the water but you cannot make him drink.

So if you're almost 30 and you're bagging groceries –is that a dream killer? I did not think so. It's honest work and there is room for growth for the person with the right attitude and foresight. As much as we parents want to live our kids' lives for them (regardless of their age), we cannot do it. It is his choice. We're his safety net during the interim and that's what parents do.

There was one Monday evening when my husband took my son to his first anger management class but lo and behold it was canceled and had been moved to Wednesday evening. No one bothered to contact those persons who were required to take this class and had signed up for this mandatory class. When my son walked in to report for the class, the person at the front desk looked up and grunted come back Wednesday at 6:30. My son told me that it made him feel as insignificant as your time is not your own. It was not considered valuable. You report to that class whenever you're told to do so. I heard the sigh of helplessness in his voice. What could a mother do? Nothing-but remind him that this is a part of the process and the system dictates to ex-offenders and remember that "this too will pass". You do the minimum time (as required per the state) and then you hope to complete your parole or probation. How anyone can successfully complete parole or probation without family support is beyond me. Everybody needs somebody to encourage them on this 'marked' journey and someone to believe in them especially when you may be at your lowest point.

I observed some interesting cases while my son was attending these classes. The arrangement was that one of us (my husband or I) had to take him to class wait in the parking lot or drive around until the class was over and then we would head back home to Arlington, Texas. These particular classes were held in Fort Worth, which is where his parole office was located. After working a full day in Fort Worth myself, I would fight the traffic home, grab a sandwich or something and we would fight the 5:30 evening westbound traffic back on Interstate 20 to Fort Worth. This went on for twelve weeks—two classes two nights per week for twelve weeks.

One of the cases I observed (while waiting one evening) was a scrappy looking couple who were cursing up a storm in their car with their windows down. Apparently she was dropping him off for the same class. If I might say so without prejudice, she appeared to have definitely been in need of the class herself. She kept pacing back and forth with jittery motions and then coming back to their car to fight physically with her husband or boyfriend or whatever. He grew tired and shouted to her "you don't even trust me to go to these d#### classes. "It's just a bunch of dope fiends" he said, "You need to trust me." Well I will say that he is wrong. My son is not a dope-phine. This was a mandated class to satisfy the conditions of his parole. Even when my son committed his offense of knocking in his girlfriend's door, the parole board must have figured that he was using something to commit an act like that. This was not so in my son's case.

There was another incident in which we arrived to the small parking lot about 5 minutes later than usual but still 20 minutes before the class started and the cars were parked crooked. Well I squeezed my husband's full size Lincoln Mark VII on the front row close to the street. I was not comfortable there but the lot was full. I did not know that I had also parked crooked. Well a dilapidated old van pulled up beside me and the guy was cussing about my parking-he didn't know that I was still in the vehicle. He looked over and saw me-raised his window and laid down. I looked at him like I was saying "what??" I never heard another word from him. I refused to take that insult inwardly. He was cursing about my driving (parking) not me. I could have rolled my eyes and asked him if there was a problem-but as I said before, he laid down. Amen. We should choose our battles wisely. That would not have been funny, if I would have gotten into an argument in the parking lot of the parole office and possibly arrested.

Things have a way of going south—in a hurry if you're not careful. I did think about what the headlines would say—mother of parolee arrested in parking lot of parole office. That would not look good. When it was my turn to take my son to class, I would remain in the car jotting down notes and ideas about this very book. Actually I was keeping a diary because this whole experience is and has been overwhelming for me and my entire family. It is impossible for me to think of myself more highly than I ought to—because it is not "those" people on parole-it's my own son who is also on parole. Please don't misread what I am saying—I never expected either of my boys to end up behind bars.

Lots of time while sitting in the parking lot waiting on him, I would look around at this Department of Corrections Parole Facility and wonder-how did I end up driving an additional 50 miles round trip two evenings per week on top of working a full time job while driving 50 miles round trip daily to my job as a housing counselor. How? You muster up strength and determination to aid your child as he or she re-enters society while seeing your own DNA within them. This is what families do. They sacrifice and support one another.

Back at the parole office I watched as the guys congregated outside the facility awaiting the start of class. My son looked so out of place. You may think that I'm being prejudicial by comparing my son to the other rough looking gentlemen. The truth is that my son, whom we affectionately nicknamed, T.J. stands out like a sore thumb. He was not supposed to be here. I was not supposed to be here with him. How did we get here? I apologize for having meltdowns periodically during the book, because we were blindsided! He's free in this chapter-but he's not free.

When individuals serve the punishment for their offenses, it is not an easy road to transition back into society. It has taken every bit of 7 weeks to receive my son's new Texas driver's license. There were a lot of hurdles just to get a new driver's license. He had already been armed with a recently renewed Illinois driver's license upon release from the Illinois institution. However since the Illinois Department of Corrections consented to allowing Texas to oversee his parole, a new Texas license would be required. When he made application for a Texas driver's license, they came real close to also requesting a pint of blood amidst all the other required documents. I am grateful for having an understanding supervisor who was flexible with me during the times where I had to serve as chauffeur to get my son to the various places in order to obtain the needed materials in a timely manner otherwise it would have been a violation of his Texas parole not to obtain such documents within the specified time period. Because the

City of Arlington has no public transportation, I did most of the running around with my son to get him recognized within the state of Texas system as a citizen. He was already recognized however as a felon in the criminal justice system. The original birth certificate that we had ever since he was born in Illinois nearly 30 years ago was not certified, so one had to be purchased online from the State of Illinois.

My son basically had to start his life all over beginning with his identification. When my son left the Illinois prison he had a picture ID with the word INMATE bold faced at the top. I was so glad when he was able to put that thing away and reclaim his identity as a regular person. When he was taken into custody in Illinois, his wallet, coat, watch and other items were put in a container at the county jail. When he was shipped off to prison, he had requested that his son's mother go claim his belongings. To make a long story short, everything that was left with her-ultimately got destroyed. After serving 3 years behind the fence, he is indeed starting from scratch.

I would encourage each of you reading this book to think twice before demeaning a family member or anyone who has ended up on the wrong side of the law and is now in the judicial system. It takes diligence and patience to help them transition to through and maneuver through many obstacles. An added burden for former inmates is the preconceived stigma which the majority of society holds toward persons who were once incarcerated.

As my son starts all over again, he is free-but not free. His ankle monitor indeed reminds me of slavery time. I am still processing this whole ordeal. During the time he was being monitored, he considered the evenings that he was attending his parole ordered classes, as a bonus. Yes – I said it! Being able to leave the house and actually step on the ground as a bonus— you can see why this chapter is called "Free But Not Free?" One day we tested this confinement system. It was grocery shopping day. I pulled the car inside the garage-so he came inside the attached garage to get the groceries out of the car as well he was able to use the exercise bench inside the garage. The time that my son spent in prison stimulated him to become and remain physically fit. My son told me that while inside the fence he bench pressed over 200 pounds. There were no rehabilitation programs per se but for only a small number of inmates so the majority of his prison sentence was spent playing basketball and lifting weights. He did not have to attend the GED classes because my son graduated high school (unlike the majority of prison inmates) and had 1 year of college working towards an Associate degree.

Some of my current clients who receive subsidized housing assistance are former inmates and some remain on probation and parole. There was an incident in which one of the clients, that is wearing an ankle monitoring device, was unable to get clearance in sufficient time from his parole officer so consequently he was not able to making his annual housing appointment. Because I personally understood what he was going through with that device, I was able to be flexible with a rescheduled appointment which I made fit within his permissible time to be outside of his apartment. This particular client had been on the monitoring device for so long (many years) and he stated to me that he was so tired of having to report to his parole office for practically every single thing. He just became a new dad and wants to spend time with his toddler daughter who just so happened to live in the same complex. He could not even go across the parking lot to visit his daughter but the mother was able to bring the child to spend time with him daily. This restrictive confinement brought tears to this parolee client's eyes when he did finally make it in for his appointment with me. Another prime example of being free, but not free. When I looked into his eyes I saw my own son's frustration. They are not alone. There are thousands of parolees and probationers who are free-not in custody yet are still in custody (not free) of their state or federal correction system. Never take your freedom for granted, because it can be taken from you in an instant. If you find yourself in a situation where you are in full control (like my son was) of the pending outcome, I encourage you to first THINK about the possible consequences of your actions. Next I ask that you RECONSIDER your probable actions. LASTLY, walk away from your probable actions by

MOTHER OF A PRISONER

REALIZING that you are not the only one who will suffer as a result of your bad or thoughtless actions should you decide to follow through on them.

I am the Mother of a Prisoner and this is my story.

REALITY CHECK VS TOUGH LOVE

I WANT SO much for my son to have the same drive as I have for him- but there's one problem –he appears not to be driven. Notice that I said 'appears'. For someone once said that things are not always they way in which they appear.

This chapter is written in the fall, in early November, roughly eighteen months after my son's release from prison and my grandson is now living with us and attending school down here. My son has not worked since May of this year. I agreed to be as transparent as possible and I am sharing with you those things which we as a family, mostly, me as the mother went through with her now former prisoner son. Not everything makes you sad and tearful of what your child or loved one has gone through since being released to the outside of the fence. Sometimes you do get angry and motherly mad (if there is such a thing). Let all the mothers reading this now attest that you have indeed gotten motherly mad at the same one you prayed for while they were incarcerated. Am I the only one?

Every time I see an e-mail about job openings during my lunch break at work I forward it to my son's e-mail address. There are times during the day when I want to call him to see if he's followed up on any of these open positions. More often than not he responds by saying, "they won't hire me, mom".

Who told you that they won't hire you? This was the basis for our recent mother/son verbal knockout punches that yes I have thrown at my own son. No one wants to talk about the Breaking Point in any family. Yes my son waited until we had pulled up roots and completely left the state of Illinois to get into serious trouble which consequently landed him in prison. Yes I was a member of two local prison ministry teams for about 6 years and my son still ended up in prison.

Now, he's out and tasting freedom for the first time since 2006 and is a full time dad. He's not the tidiest person and has been without work for seven long months. I have lost count of the heated verbal exchanges between my son and me, but the most recent one cut pretty deep.

Since my 7 year old grandson has come to live with us I get a chance to observe my son's parenting skills. Some days are worse than others. Just today after getting home from work and coming through the kitchen and seeing left over dish water in the sink, drain board loaded with dishes needing to be put away. I call this the landslide. Dishes will air dry in less than 30 minutes and then they should be put away to make room for the soon to come food preparation dishes for the next meal of the day. I believe it was mentioned in an earlier chapter that I have some OCD issues (obsessive compulsory disorder) behavioral issues. I have not talked with any psychologist but I work with enough social workers and case managers and I have diagnosed myself. I cannot start a meal with dirty dishes or dirty dish water left in the sink and water all over the counter. I have a large kitchen with dishwasher-which is only used 4 or 5 times per year. It uses too much water is my reason for not being used more and it has leaked.

What I believe and I shared this with my son is that he does not plan his days. I guess I want him to be the male version of me—sounds funny? Not so. I was between jobs for eighteen months several years ago and I know it is a job looking for a job. Yes, my son has a felony on his record, yet I expect him to contact those places which specifically advertise that criminal backgrounds considered if under seven years. I need clarification of whether it's seven years from sentencing day or seven years from the release day or seven years from the arrest. I want him to contact his parole officer or the re-entry office first for understanding and then contact the employer. I am an eternal optimist and am still praying for my son. I have even made him a list of celebrities which have felonies on their records as well as biblical characters that spent time in jail hoping to raise his self esteem because he is in really good company.

I want him to be motivated. What he is currently doing is taking my grandson to school and picking him up. After school he makes sure he has a snack and immediately they get into the homework. This was a good routine and I was pleased and my grandson's grades did reflect it. What I, the helicopter mom, wanted was for him to try to find any job that he could work during the school hours and of course would not interfere in his picking up my grandson from school. There were a couple of days during the week that my husband would be able to trade off if for some reason the hours were staggered. Doesn't that sound like a perfect plan? Of course it does—but he was not able to find that perfect job which fit that perfect time slot.

So the motherly mad trait conceded and thought 'if you can't find a job during the perfect school day slot, the house should be spotless every day and what about having dinner at least started?' The thing is that we women expect men (and sons) to volunteer to do the obvious. It does not happen. What does it take to motivate him? He didn't have to do anything to the master suite-just the common areas of the house which he and my grandson occupy. He took care of doing their laundry and putting away their clothes.

I do not want to coddle him. I want to love him even when he's unlovable. Seems like I have heard that somewhere before. What about the bible, Christ loved and loves us when we were/are unlovable. It seems to infuriate my son when I point things our or make suggestions regarding his progress regarding job searches. How about something reasonable like tracking your own efforts-making a list of companies that you contacted and the response you received. I never asked to see his list. He needs to gauge his own efforts and the only way you can do this is with a contact list of places which you have sought employment either by going to the business or applying on line.

My son never reminded me of his three year hiatus when we got into our heated verbal exchanges. After cooling off periods, I would ease up and give him space. Remember that I gave my son two months off when he was initially released so now that Release Vacation time is over. I don't want him to lose sight of the competition. Because the economy has stalled, I would automatically remind him of May and December college graduates that would also be in the market and I've heard that some college graduates are trying to get any job they can. I had to remind him that because of the graduate competition he must be vigilant in his job seeking. I believe the Lord rewards our efforts—not our idleness or wishful thinking. We can wish for a job until the choir stops singing, but you must get up and do something. I believe my son finally got it. He realizes that it is a job looking for a job. Tough love is tough on the receiver and tougher on the giver, but it must be done.

Now when I get home he comes to me and reports how many contacts he made that day. I am so proud of his efforts and I know something is going to happen for him real soon.

I am the Mother of a Prisoner and this is my story.

SECOND CHANCE

IT IS AN understatement to merely 'say' that everybody deserves a second chance. Until I went through this experience with my own son, I never expected such hypocrisy especially in high places and close places. Let's start with the close places, the people that are closest to you have no idea how an incarcerated loved one changes your life and your family. Yet if you ask anybody on the street whether they felt that an incarcerated person who has paid their debt to society deserves a second chance, mind you, they will respond with a resounding 'Yes'—this is what America is all about. Au contraire, as they say in French—quite the contrary.

Earlier this week I was reading commentaries on author Michelle Alexander's book, "The New Jim Crow." The online newspaper in a particular city also prints comments that anyone can go online and inject their feelings on a subject—no matter how vile it is. The comments made by the locals concerning the speaker's comparison of the inequity of the current judicial system and the rate of incarcerated black males, were just downright nasty. The author stated that the number of black males incarcerated in this country far exceeds the population of some of our major cities.

The gross disparity between black males and white males being incarcerated for the same offense is very disheartening. I am not dealing the race component at this point, please bear with me and read on. However there was a lot of bitterness expressed in the majority of those e-mails. Such statements were 'hey you do the crime, you must do the time', 'nobody told you to make bad choices', 'when they are released-let them come live next door to you.' Lock'em up and throw away the key; 'in a few years-your own son will probably join you there-settle down and wait for your kid, homeboy'. This is just a mere glimpse of the harsh and sometimes racist attitudes towards persons who have unfortunately turned down the wrong walkway of life and are trying to find their way back to society.

I must make this statement here and now which will be repeated in some fashion throughout the book, because it forces individuals to dare search themselves and be bold enough to say either audibly or internally—what would I do if this happened to me? How would I feel if my son or daughter was suddenly arrested, denied a decent job, was shunned by society and even persons in their family's 'inner circle' with the label of 'felon' which will now follow you for the rest of your life. How would you feel? You would not be so quick to say such horrendous things that are regularly mentioned in public commentaries.

I want to review my own early conceptions of what should happen to prisoners upon release. As a child, I don't recall any of my immediate family members being caught up in the judicial system. During high school I do remember a new kid at our school that shot a gas station attendant to death and of course he went to jail. I remember in junior high school we took a tour of the county jail—this was a direct attempt to discourage us from engaging in a life of crime-this would be equated to a small town version of a recent reality series called 'Scared Straight'. It worked for me personally. All I can remember is that the jail was dark-dingy and smelly. As a young teenager—I made a decision that this was one place that I never wanted to end up. But as a young person, my thoughts were purely selfish—this is where 'I' don't want to end up. I do not recall thinking twice about the future of those individuals who did end up in jail. If a person is truly transparent, their own suppressed feelings will surface.

There are several political highlights and 'firsts' that have occurred while penning this book. They include the election and re-election of the first African American President of the United States of America, Barack H. Obama; the capture of terrorist and murderer, Sadaam Hussein, who was eventually killed by his own people; the killing of Osama Bin Laden, the known mastermind behind the September 11 bombings in New York City, the first woman, Nancy Pelosi, to serve as Speaker of the House and the first female Hispanic Supreme Court Justice, Sonia Sotomayor. One final sad highlight which also took place while penning this book was the death of political prisoner and international hero, Nelson Mandela. After spending twenty-seven years in a South African prison, he rose to become the first black South African president. He died in December 2013.

During the first election of President Obama my son was still incarcerated in the President's home state of Illinois. At the time of the re-election in 2012, he was out, living in Texas with us but did not make an attempt to vote because he had been told that ex-felons could not vote. Throughout the last presidential election there were numerous billboards (mostly in the northeast) which targeted ex-felons, some even daring them to show up at polling place to vote. The political motives of such groups which paid thousands and thousands of dollars for such racially charged target marketing (because those billboards were strategically placed in predominantly black and Hispanic neighborhoods), will not be speculated by me, yet it is definitely personal. Our formerly incarcerated son's not voting slipped by my husband and me. This right must be tested if not by my son, then by me as a concerned citizen using the right of inquiry of whether ex-felons can in fact vote in the great state of Texas. The reason that it fell from underneath our radar was that during the last Presidential election our son had moved out of the house prior to November 6, 2012 election day.

But who did accompany me on that historic election day was my nine year old grandson—so in a way my son was present 'through' my grandson, little Theo, whom I let push the button for me while standing alongside of me in the voting booth. As a result, America had decided to give President Barack Obama a Second Chance as the most powerful leader in the free world.

However, in the context of my book, Second Chance refers to the legislation which was originally signed into law by former President George W. Bush in April 2008. The formal name is the Second Chance Act. It is the first- of- its kind legislation which authorizes various grants to government agencies and nonprofit groups to provide employment assistance, substance abuse treatment, mentoring, victim's support and other services that can help reduce re-offending and violations of probation and parole. In layman's terms the act was created to help the hundreds and thousands of formerly incarcerated persons released from prisons and jail to make a positive and productive transition back to their communities and hopefully help stop the revolving door back to the jail/prison facilities.

Please don't think that this piece of legislation just sailed through both houses of the Congress and landed on the president's desk for an immediate signature. No, the Act was actually named in 2007 but after many committee and subcommittee meetings, hearings and witness testimonials , reconsideration, postponement of voting and reintroduction, the Second Chance Act language was finally acceptable by enough members in both houses to get it out of committee and actually placed for vote on the floors of both houses. I am not a politician, so some steps have been abbreviated in order to make my point. No matter how good an idea is, no matter how moral a process is, to assist individuals get 'back on track' with their lives and the lives of their families, gridlock does exist. One ray of sunshine is eminent and hope does prevail.

As of this writing, the Second Chance Reauthorization Act of 2013, S.1690/H.R. 3465 is pending in Congress. According to the ASCA(Association of State Correctional Administrators) this reauthorization would extend the prisoner reentry programs for an additional five years, including grants, mentoring, substance abuse and family-based planning. This new bill, the Second Chance Reauthorization Act of 2013 was introduced in the Senate by Leahy and Portman and in the House by several Congressmen including Davis, Sensenbrenner,

Fudge and others. I plan to ask my own senators and congressmen to support this vital measure. Hopefully before this book is published, this important piece of legislation will have the support of the total Congress. Attorney General Eric Holder endorsed the reauthorization of the Second Chance Act in November of 2013 and encouraged the Congress to pass this bipartisan legislation.

My son, along with hundreds of thousands of other FI's, (former inmates), definitely deserve another opportunity to again be productive citizens of society. I can hear someone saying 'how do you know whether that individual was a productive member of society in the first place before landing in the penal system?' Rightly so I don't. Let's rephrase it by saying in general everyone who has been in prison, done his or her time, paid their debt to society has the right of redemption. Additionally, if they have never been on Straight street they should be given a chance to join in and grasp the revelation of wanting to do the right thing perhaps for the first time in their lives since early childhood.

My friends, this is what being given a Second Chance is all about. I am sure as you are reading this book you can think of at least 2 or 3 instances where you were forgiven for something you did and the person or persons involved welcomed you with open arms and allowed you to get back in the game and resume the play, if you will. Even if was not to the degree where you exited the game—the fact is 'you're back in the game'. That is exactly what a person who was formerly incarcerated wants—to be allowed to get back in the game and be given a Second chance.

Talk is cheap- Agreed? Here comes the hypocrisy. Let's use the example where your family or your organization has a FI (former inmate) in your midst but not everyone is displaying the spirit of a Second Chance. Sure people say the politically correct thing publicly, 'or course we'll give you a Second Chance', but their actions are far opposite from their verbal admissions. Your infraction, mistake, offense or crime is constantly being thrown up in your face and perhaps you are the topic of many gossip circles, text messages, recrimination, negative Facebook post and other social media comments made about you.

How many people actually take time to really talk with a FI (former inmate) to see how are they doing or ask what can I do to help? I believe that unless they are a paid staffer, the number is probably not that great. What is my basis for this? How about seven years in an active volunteer church prison ministry group where out of a congregation of hundreds only the faithful 4 or 5 members for years at a time get in their own vehicles and drive to prisons to greet, minister and encourage persons who have ended up behind bars. Perhaps you say well I give regular donations to my church's prison ministry. From my personal conversation with inmates, they almost always say that "when I get out of this place, I will join a church that has an active prison ministry." The people behind the bars are starved for interaction with those of us on the outside. They were so starved in Illinois, the few times when we could not make it due to heavy snowfall and dangerous road conditions; they were actually disappointed in us. Seriously.

There is a saying that when a person gets married, they're not just marrying one individual, they are in fact marrying the whole family. Same difference with a FI (former inmate)-sometimes the whole family is made to feel as if they also committed the same crime along with their loved one. This is Double Jeopardy at its worst.

The saving grace behind our personal situation is that my husband and I had already relocated to Texas before this incident ever occurred with my son, who was still living alone in Illinois. All of the friends which we had made over the 30 years of living in central Illinois, no one made direct contact with us when my son's name hit the local newspaper. I received one e-mail the day after the arrest charges of home invasion, criminal trespass and domestic battery were made public in the local newspaper against my son. If our family was being shunned or defamed-it was being done out of our presence in another state.

It has been a difficult road for my eldest son since his release from prison in 2009; the most challenging is finding employment. A vast number of men behind bars have little or no education not even a GED. My son however entered the judicial system not only with a high school diploma but, was on the road to getting his Associates' Degree in Construction Engineering when he took a detour and let his emotions run amuck. To encourage employers to hire individuals with a background, included in the original legislation were tax credits to those employers for doing the right thing by giving qualified FI's (former inmates) an opportunity to take care of themselves and their families by re-entering the workplace and actually getting a job.

On practically all job applications there is a dedicated box or line or two requiring the applicant to answer whether they have either ever been arrested and/ or if you have a felony, please explain. Then what follows is the politically correct statement which goes something like this–just because you have a background does not necessarily mean that you are automatically disqualified for consideration for employment. I always told my son that you must tell the truth. During my son's three years on parole, he never received role play (oral or written) of how to respond to having a felony on your record when on a job interview. Now there are some re-entry services that do generalize situations, but with a felony, which my son does have, responses need to be so articulated to ensure that his application warrants a second look by that person or persons who are reviewing the applications. I also told my son and this goes for anybody looking for a job—you need to have in your brain or in your heart at least three reasons why any employer should hire you. What do you have to offer?

I was and still am a' hard' life coach/mother but I wanted him to know that you are competing against people with college degrees even some with Master degrees who are out of work and are desperately looking for employment. I reminded him that he does have an edge; that Jesus Christ is on your side and of course you have my DNA. (I'm not being sacrilegious-please don't judge me) My son is out of the house now and he did wrestle with his answers to possible interview questions, but as I told him certain questions can only be answered by you.

I have tried to encourage my son as I did for others while serving for years on the prison ministry team-to hold your head up; you have done your time. You have my DNA so put one foot in front of the other and step to get your life back. If the Lord himself can grant you a second chance third chance and more, why can't other people allow you to get on the Second Chance train of recapturing your life?

It would be a gross oversight if I did not make this statement that not everyone incarcerated is guilty of that crime which landed them in the judicial system, whereas some are not guilty of any crime. That is true whether you choose to believe it or not. Were it not true, then how do you explain so many quote victims have since recanted their allegations ten, twenty, twenty-five, thirty years after an innocent person has spent the most productive part of their lifetime, their children's lifetime inside a 7 x 9 cell? No I don't have the exact number of innocent people behind bars that have been set free and it may not be a statistic that is readily available, but for sure on a state level especially where that state or jurisdiction has an active chapter of the Innocence Project that is functioning and funded either by grants or donations. On that same note, most of the men which have been set free and declared not guilty have been able to collect a financial settlement from that state. That in itself should be recorded somewhere because that money for wrongful incarceration would have to come from that city's or state's budget.

As I bring this chapter to a close I challenge my readers not to sympathize with former inmates (FI's) but try to empathize with what they may be going through as they try to rebuild their lives. Give them a second chance. The songwriter, Joe South, put it well in the song "Walk a Mile in My Shoes", "before you abuse, criticize and accuse, just walk a mile in my shoes." Truthfully speaking, most of us (including myself) would not be able to endure what FI's went through behind the fence. Whereas the poet and author, Dr. Rebera Elliott Foston , has so eloquently stated in her infamous poem *"You Don't Live On*

My Street", how could you possibly know what a FI or the family of a FI goes through when you don't live where they live (not always referring to real estate) . The families in these spectrums are asking for one thing 'acceptance'. This is what I, the *Mother of a Prisoner*, am asking you to accept the person, not the offense which may have been committed. Now in case there are some extremists that are fuming while reading this particular chapter, I am compelled to at least comment on this looming question: Does EVERY criminal deserve a Second Chance, regardless of the crime? With all personal interests aside, I would have to say YES. This is the reason why the American judicial system is one of the greatest systems in the world. Perfect-of course not. I believe that if every criminal that has stood before the judge-has accepted and served their time and have demonstrated to the various parole/probation boards that they are no longer a threat to society—they should be granted a second chance in society.

A second chance in some cases may come with harsh restrictions depending on the severity of the offense, the number of victims involved, the remorse of the convicted person and other factors as determined by the review board. I'm also not naïve enough to say that some offenses are so horrendous and carried life in prison or the death penalty, then that unfortunately would negate receiving a second chance. Now if this individual decides to become a repeat offender and lands back behind prison walls (called recidivism), the opportunity of getting another chance would not be automatic. The bar has to be raised with additional requirements set in place. God forbid, if my son were to end up back behind bars—justice would be discharged to him like any other repeat offender for the same offense.

As I had mentioned in an earlier paragraph about the voting rights of former inmates, I took the time to investigate which states do allow FI's (former inmates) the right to vote. Without singling out each state, I will merely highlight the two states which were directly involved with my son's incarceration, Illinois, where my son was imprisoned and the state of Texas where he spent his parole years. In Illinois, individuals incarcerated for a felony conviction are ineligible to vote.

However voting rights are automatically restored upon release from prison. People on parole or probation can vote in the state of Illinois. Therefore ex-offenders should re-register to vote.

In August 2013, according to an article in Progress Illinois, the governor of Illinois, Gov. Pat Quinn, signed legislation that is slated to give ex-offenders in Illinois a Second chance at employment and a productive life. Gov. Quinn noted that more than 50% of Illinois inmates return to prison within three years. I am so glad that my son fell in the 49% of those that do not return to prison. He completed his parole successfully. The tax credit to Illinois employers is slated to more than double in a state bill for those employers who hire qualified inmates within three years of being released from jail. Such employers can take that credit for up to five years.

According to the Texas Secretary of State's website, a convicted felon can vote in Texas as long as the sentence has been fully discharged in terms of incarceration, parole, supervision or completed a period of probation ordered by any court or has been pardoned. Upon hearing this news, I can barely wait to let my son know that he can re-register to vote. There are three states in our country, according to ACLU's Map of State Felony Disfranchisement Laws, where convicted felons' rights to vote are permanently disallowed- Florida, Kentucky and Iowa. Perhaps a citizens' movement may develop and pressure placed on their lawmakers to take a second look at their own laws. With this permanency, hundreds of thousands of voters' voices and interests are silenced forever. The other state laws vary in ranges.

I hope if your heart has been softened and you want to be proactive, the Second Chance Act Renewal or Reauthorization legislation is not an automatic hands down common sense vote by the United States Congress. The supporters are always looking for individuals to sign on-line petitions as well as to contact their senators and representatives for continued sponsorship. The National Reentry Resource Center is a continual beacon of information on this topic and has a monthly newsletter. If there is any further interest please go to nationalreentryresourcecenter.org . We're hoping that since the current Congress which has unfortunately been labeled the least productive Congress in the history of these United States, will do what is necessary to restore funding for this legislation again.

Just before concluding this chapter, I visited the above website to see if there had been any movement on the bill and there has been. As late as last week, January 17, 2014, the Congress did send the funding bill to the President which includes 27 billion dollars for criminal justice. Under this bill, the Second Chance Act would receive $67.7 million in funding. Much appreciation to the Congress and now it's on the President's desk. I will not comment on the breakdown of the Second Chance Act funding, again visit the above website for more details. If you would like to see how the senators and representatives representing your state voted, that information is also public record.

Prisoners also can be of benefit to persons on the outside while they themselves are still on the inside of the fence. There was one particular inmate who is serving time as a convicted murderer (he was the accomplice) whose actions, while still incarcerated, came to the rescue of a family in Colorado who young son is autistic. As reported in March 2014 on the ABC Evening National News this particular convict has been training service dogs for some time but he went a step further and self-taught himself to specifically train service dogs to deal with autistic children. Please note this is not common place for service animals to specialize in. According to the article this inmate researched the prison library for every article or book he could get his hands on for this specialty training. Apparently there is a current trend in prisoners training dogs for general service, this one stood out above the rest.

What happens is the dog's presence helps the autistic child sleep at night and learns to sense the child's growing anxiety and the dog breaks that mood by either touching, nudging, licking the child whatever the dog can do to get the child out of that anxiety mode and back on the regular mode of behavior.

Prior to this nine year old child's interaction with this incarcerated inmate, he would not let anyone touch him. After a while, the dog learned this child's behavior and according to the parents the results have been remarkable.

The child was being transported 200 miles to work with this dog at the prison. The kids don't necessarily see the prisoners while during this interactive training with the service animal. These parents had made a mission out of helping their son and they were so pleased with the results that they wanted to meet this inmate. The meeting was arranged with prison personnel. Not only were the parents able to personally thank this inmate, the autistic boy, who would not let anyone touch him, was able to shake this inmate's hand with delight. The parents said in that interview that prison was the last place which they imagined where help would be found for their son. The parents also said that the prisoner had proved that he could make a difference in some else's life and that he did. This is just one of many instances where we are forced to realize that prisoners are people too. While this particular inmate might not be getting out soon if at all, his dedicated over the top training with that dog has changed that family's life forever. Everyone on this earth was created to do something special and make a deposit in the earth and this inmate found his on the inside of a prison facility.

The same personal drive displayed by this inmate as well as thousands of others is what I have tried to instill in both of my sons, especially the one who spent 3 years on the inside of a state prison.

I am the Mother of a Prisoner and this is my story.

ONE YEAR LATER

SOMETIMES IT SEEMS as if time is standing still. I continually look up at the sky or ceiling or just staring into space and I wonder-how did this happen? Amazingly on the other hand, time has gone by and it is now one year later. One year later when we waited in the cold Illinois February temperature for our son to walk out of the prison a free man again. Oh my God! It feels so good to have him here with us.

My son recently celebrated one year of being released from prison. He is now on parole, more commonly referred to as being "on paper" for the remaining two years. In the words of the Corrections Department- he is 'under supervision".

After twelve long, soul-searching, job-hunting and rejection hearing months on the outside, my son is considered a parolee. Please note that this reference is one that I never dreamed of that would impact my own family. As a mother I do consider this event a milestone in my own life. The rate of recidivism (when a person returns to prison) is supposedly very high for almost any kind of offender. Such details, percentages and statistics will be covered in the chapter "My Son Is Not a Statistic".

As I look back during this month of February 2010, my soul is rejoicing because my son is home. Just like the father of the prodigal son said in the Bible "-Rejoice! My son is home."(Luke 15:11-32). My son has still not opened up to me fully and I am sure he had some 'moments' on the inside of the fence. Those moments will also be covered in a later chapter. It has been and is still very difficult for my son to walk with his head up and not constantly looking over his shoulders. I'm not a psychologist, but this trait is indicative of what my son went through during his time in prison. One day I asked him about why the look of uneasiness even when he was with me, he said that when he was in 'the joint' you had to always be aware of who was nearby and always be on alert because a situation could creep up at any time. It did not matter whether you were directly involved or not, you could have just been too close to a geographical radius of an incident and you get labeled that you were involved which could cost you additional time on top of your original sentence. You might say what can they do to a prisoner who is found guilty of breaking the rules on the inside? Well this situation almost happened to my son.

He was sentenced to one of the better correctional facilities in Illinois (which is what I prayed for) but a situation almost cost him to be deported out to another facility and heaven knows what could have happened at another location. My son spent his entire sentence at a medium security facility. As a result of being misidentified on one occasion as an inmate who started a fight –my son was almost sent to a maximum security facility. This would have been a nightmare-a place where you sleep with your eyes open. It could have been a place where the body odor is so extreme because you were either too afraid to bathe (without a buddy on the lookout) or bathing privileges had been suspended due to perhaps being on lockdown.

Lockdown refers to when the entire facility or portion of the facility is shut off from the outside world due to a serious infraction of the rules (ex. inmate fighting, contraband suspected, etc). No one is allowed to move around or leave their cells. No phone calls during lockdown, no commissary privileges (which meant if you did not already have snacks or munchies or personal hygiene items stored up- you had to go lacking).

Now that my son is out of prison, he is very distant and doesn't talk much about the three years spent inside. Because of this book, he has indeed opened up to me, the writer, not so much to me, the mother. I know he feels ashamed, but the frustration of not being able

ONE YEAR LATER

to get a job greatly exceeds the shame. As a mother of a prisoner, I will probably never know all that my son went through during his incarceration, but I want him to know that ANYTIME he wants to talk about it, I am ready to listen.

Texas, like many other states, does have re-entry programs in several cities. For some reason my son has shied away from relying on this program for resources and job leads. I believe that he has been to the local re-entry office probably three times since his release. Two appointments with that office were a prerequisite of getting your hands on the much coveted job list which was supposed to include companies who were open to hiring persons with backgrounds and had actually hired felons in the past. When my son finally got 'that' list, it had been copied so many times that there was hardly any ink left on the pages thereby being unreadable. He was so excited and began calling on the companies at my insistence. I had coached him on updating his resume' and rehearsed tough interview questions with him. He applied on line with many companies. Immediately the companies he contacted from that list said 'No felons'. What a letdown! This list was supposed to be golden. What do you mean –no felons?? But you're on the list is what I said silently and I'm sure that's what he felt like telling them.

It hurt me almost as much as it did him to see the rejection by employers. This type of disappointment was so hurtful until he stopped going to the local re-entry office altogether. Unfortunately my son feels that the staff of the re-entry office was just following a script with no hope attached to it. They were doing what they were told to do. I pleaded with my son to keep the communication lines open with the re-entry office because they would be the recipients of governmental grants and announcements to hopefully still aid in him obtaining employment.

At this particular time, and even to this day, the City of Arlington, Texas had no viable mean of public transportation at all except for disabled individuals. This made the task of reporting to his parole officer (who was in Fort Worth) more difficult as well as stopping by the

Texas Re-Entry Services office which was also in Fort Worth almost an impossible task. Some mornings, with clearance from his parole office I would take him to the Re-entry office and /or the parole office drop him off and I would return to work and wait for his call to be picked up. I am grateful that my supervisor did flex my working time, when I had to run anywhere on behalf of my paroled son. When he finished his appointments in Fort Worth, my supervisor would allow me to drive him back home to Arlington and then I would return back to work at Forth Worth. Please note that she was flexible, however this absence time was coded as paid time off (PTO) as far as payroll is concerned.

Arlington, Texas is the largest city in America without any viable means of public transportation, excluding limited services for the disabled. Being the mother of a 'former' prisoner who is now a parolee with no means of public transportation is taxing on the whole family. We did what we had to do until he was able with the help of a friend to get his own vehicle. We love our son, but because we had paid for an attorney who unfortunately was not able to get his case dismissed, we could not afford to get him a car at this time. We have two vehicles however my husband and I work in different cities. Finding out that there was no public transportation in a city of this size (over 300,000 people) was really a shocker. This meant that our son was totally dependent on me and my husband to travel anywhere which was not in walking distance. We have heard local people say public transportation has been on the ballot and voted down twice, prior to us moving to Arlington.

When my son first arrived here in Texas to live with us after his Illinois ordeal, I said to myself that because of all that he had been through I would allow him to take off a couple of months and just relax. He could sleep in on the mornings when his dad and I had to get up every day to get ready for work. He had the run of the whole house, three television sets, stereo, computer, exercise equipment and a refrigerator full of food that he could eat whatever he wanted to whenever he wanted to. As the mother of a prisoner, I believe that during these months of 'chilling' he played over and over in his mind just how he ended up in prison in the first place.

After the chilling period was over, I felt that in addition to us having to get him to the group classes (anger management and substance abuse) which were a part of his parole, it was time for him to update his resume' and start knocking on some doors and get employment. Besides, he was still a father whose young son remained in Illinois. He had to come up with a way to earn some money to help with the expenses of being a dad. When he was first released from prison, he was not allowed to immediately join us in Texas. He was initially paroled to his son's mother's home in central Illinois for almost 30 days with an ankle monitor on. I thought everything was set for him to complete his parole in Texas where we were now living. Truthfully I was afraid for him being out of prison, still in Illinois (out of mother's reach), while we were back in Texas. I had rejoiced in the fact that he was indeed out of prison yet on edge about him but still alone in the state which had incarcerated him, due to some incomplete paperwork between the Illinois and Texas Departments of Corrections. After 30 days he did join us in Texas by way of a Greyhound bus, and I was so relieved.

I never expected him to have such an awful hard time finding a job. I had not read the memo about the mark of a felon on your record. I still take issue with that to this day, because this was MY son, my DNA, he looks like me and I was in prison ministry for 7 years in the state of Illinois. He finished high school, even attended junior college. How could MY son be subjected to the same treatment as other felons? I was a Godly woman and a praying woman and I believed God that my son would get a job and if he applied himself he would move on and up in life. Faith without works is still dead. He would still have to apply himself. He would have to show some effort. All the praying in the world would not have the job come knocking on his door. He would have to get up and do the knocking. Ask and it will be given, Seek and you will find Knock and the door will be opened (Matthew 7:7).

The lack of public transportation in Arlington has already been mentioned, so my son walked over a mile to a small strip mall which had 8 restaurants (including four fast foods) and an estimated 12 – 13 retail stores, home improvement store, pet sore, plus banks and barber shops. Surely someone would give my son an opportunity, even if it was janitorial-Right? It was within walking distance from our home.

He is a fast walker with long legs; he could be at that location even after having to cross a busy Southbound and Northbound highway within 20 minutes. It would take longer in the scorching Texas heat. My son also told me about the memo that felons won't be hired in retail establishments. I was in real estate sales for 16 years, so 'No' to me meant 'not now'—it was not a 'permanent' no. Too bad, my son did not have my drive—he was discouraged after getting 3 no's. I can understand he's been locked away for 3 years and emerged with little or no self confidence. He apparently has forgotten that there is nothing too hard for the Lord. This is one of several prayer requests that I have put on the altar.

As a mother, when your child hurts, you hurt. When your son gets discouraged, you get discouraged. The difference is I couldn't stay discouraged and I didn't want him to see me crying over all the hard job seeking time that he was going through. He did land a sales job with a home improvement team in North Texas- but was let go a week or so later when one of the higher ups got wind of my son's background which he disclosed in black and white on the job application. This is strange, because every application has that dreaded line about are you a felon and how old is the offense. Most applications also include the politically correct disclaimer something like this, if you are a felon, this does not mean that you are automatically excluded from employment consideration. The application would also go on to say 'please use a separate sheet of paper to comment on the felony offense and list the date(s) of the offense'.

In my son's case, we talked about this when I was serving as his employment coach. I gave him the sample verbiage which he could use when applying for a job. What was equally difficult was his resume' which showed a 3 year gap in employment which has to be explained.

He had only received one interview at one of the fast foods places at the strip mall near our home, but never got a call back. It seems like every day he was sinking lower and lower with regards to his attitude and self –esteem. Every day when I got home I would ask how many places you contacted that day. I could tell by me doing this daily, it was making him feel even worse, so I eased up a little on him. It was rough. It was a delicate balance-to comfort and encourage him during all the no's, while at the same time pushing him gently to keep moving, don't give up, something's got to give. He finally landed a telemarketing job as well as a job selling vacuum cleaners. You bet you I bought a $1000 vacuum cleaner from my son and it had all the bells and whistles. I am mechanically challenged so I depended on him to vacuum and shampoo my carpet regularly as well as use those fancy attachments to dust and do all the other things it was designed to do. He was a terrific salesman because I was a tough customer and I really did not want to pay that much for a vacuum cleaner. He worked very hard but we didn't know that when the manager negotiated the price that discounted amount came out of my son's commission check and on the few weeks that he worked there—he practically was working for free.

Things have got to get better. They must. Six Flags Amusement Park, downtown Arlington had a 3 day hiring fair and we went there. We weren't sure how he would make it downtown to work but he applied anyway. Again not even a call back from an amusement park? ! My son wanted to become Construction Engineer-twelve hours short of an Associate's Degree and he could not get work flipping burgers or cleaning up the rides and grounds at an amusement park? Are you kidding me?! Now if you are not a believer-these next statements do not apply to you-you may skip it and start on the next paragraph. I am my brother's keeper. I'm concerned about his needs. I'm concerned about his struggles and I want to help him. Who is my brother?

Anybody that has a need which I can help fill is my brother.

Surely my son is not the only felon in north Texas that doesn't have a job or any transportation. What are felons supposed to do? How are they supposed to feed their families? I would hope that an uncivilized person doesn't respond and say something as ridiculous and selfish as 'they should have never done the crime.' Only a moron would say something like that –a person oblivious to the reason why we have a judicial system to make individuals (such as my son) accountable for their actions. The elephant in the room is after a person has paid their debt to society we (as a nation) continue to make them pay over and over again by denying them employment to survive and support their families. Then you get some quack from an outrageous far left extremist group that takes a scripture out of context by saying if a man won't work he will not eat. Hey—my son wanted to work but no one would hire him and give him a chance- also he is not eligible to receive food stamps to help feed his child. What is wrong with this picture? Everything! Thankfully, my husband and I are in a position to fill in that gap until some employer is open-minded enough to give our son a chance to work and prove him worthy and capable of holding down a job.

There are hundreds probably thousands of ex-felons who may have been alienated by their families and the system itself; who want to work, cannot get a job, cannot get food stamps, who are forced to do the unthinkable— contribute to the recidivism rate and commit another crime and go back through that revolving door in order to get 3 meals a day and a bed. Again something is terribly wrong with this picture.

We spoke about the 'no retail jobs for felons' memo which I am still not receiving in my spirit-however my son has embraced this mindset and unfortunately, there is nothing I can do to change his mind. Being the overbearing mother that I am, during the first few months of his release I did not bug him about looking for a job. I wanted him to enjoy the peace and quiet of being at home, sleeping in a clean bed using his private bathroom without having someone else present in the room while you do your 'business'. I also wanted him to enjoy chewing his food not having to rush through his meal like he did at the chow hall-get indigestion and back in line for your cell block to return to your housing unit. I wanted my son to remember again what a good night's sleep feels like and to actually see the trees, hear the birds sing and see the squirrels store up the acorns for the winter. Now that the ankle monitor is off, he could walk down the streets without having to always look over his shoulder. This is life.

One year later I am now able to speak more freely about the fact that yes I have a son who did time in prison. Yes he paid his debt to society and is trying to move on with his life. It is true that time is a great healer and great strengthener. I would never have entertained the fact that : a) we moved from Illinois in the fall of 2004 after 30 years of residency , and b) the following Spring of 2005 our son would be booked and charged with an incident which blindsided though not derailed our entire family including his only son and our only grandson. He was facing a 30 year prison term! Who would have thought that one year later in 2006 a judge would sentence my son to 6 years in prison? Life certainly has some crooks and turns valleys as well as hills and mountains.

One year later after his release, my son has exhaled and now it is time to remember that just because of his 3 year absence from his son, who is also his namesake, he still has responsibilities as a father and still has a monthly parole fee that he must pay. Every year on February 9th, I recall when the prison doors swung open and my son walked out a free (but not free) man under supervision of the state. My son took a detour from his destiny through an Illinois state prison. A detour does not necessarily mean that you won't get to your destination, it may take longer, but you will still get to your destiny. My son will be able to tell his own story what it's really like on the other side of the fence. In a later chapter, I actually sit down with my son and do a very candid interview of what life was like for him on the inside.

Those of you who have a child, relative or friend incarcerated, keep this in mind if you can just make it through the first year-you will make it. Now the first year may seem like it's taking forever, but with the help of the Lord, family support and staying in touch with your incarcerated loved one, time does eventually move on.

Those of us on the outside must stay strong and continue to encourage those on the inside.

I am the Mother of a Prisoner and this is my story.

ONE ON ONE INTERVIEW WITH MY SON, THE FORMER INMATE (FI)

EVEN THOUGH THIS is my story, I felt it necessary for my son's own words to be heard on these pages so that you, the reader, can hear for yourself the voice of a former inmate. (FI) This interview took place at my home in Texas the day after Memorial Day 2013, four years after my son's release from prison. My son was off that day and I had just gotten home from work myself about 30 minutes before he arrived. I had prayed about the exact questions to ask yet deep inside I wondered if I was ready for what my own son had to say. Some of his remarks are pretty graphic and some have been slightly modified for the sake of the overall context of the book. In this dialogue I represented myself as a journalist and not a mother, which was very difficult to do on some of the questions.

Question: In your lifetime based on things that you've heard or movies that you've seen or conversations that you've had with some of your friends, did you EVER imagine that you would end up in jail one day?

Answer (TJ)-Yes it was one of my biggest fears. I kept seeing it on TV, at the movies; a lot of my boys had friends and cousins that were being picked up like nobody's business. I thought that man, one of these days I may have to deal with something. Things in the newspapers are made to look worse that they actually are.

Question: When did it hit you that you might get some prison time after first being sent to the county jail?

Answer (TJ) -It wasn't until after the bench trial and I was on the bus from the courthouse returning back to the county jail—I thought to myself 'damn I might not get out of here for a while.' My attorney had led me as well as ya'll to believe that their (the prosecution's) case was weak- and I had nothing to worry about. But now 3 years inside and 3 years later on parole—we see where that was not the case.

Question: What would you attribute as the misstep which landed you in jail and ultimately in prison?

Answer (TJ) - Unfortunately mom, you know I've always had a temper. Even when I got arrested I didn't take it seriously and neither did I take the law seriously. I really didn't think that my charge would be that bad. I definitely did not think that what happened between me and my girlfriend was that severe—it was a lover's quarrel—nobody got hit-nobody got hurt but the State of Illinois came after me with guns blazing! They went straight by the book on my case. I thought the justice system would do a case by case—but not in my situation. I'm living it.

Question: When were you the most scared while in prison?

Answer (TJ) - I was never really scared -cause I knew I could take care of myself. I was more upset than scared. I'm not trying to sound tough but knowing that I would not be going home soon, I told myself that I cannot be scared-everybody's watching you. I thought about everything that I worked hard for and now I'm waking up to a gray wall. I seriously did not and still to this day think that my actions deserved that type of punishment to end up with a felony on my record for life!

ONE ON ONE INTERVIEW WITH MY SON, THE FORMER INMATE (FI)

Question: Describe a typical day while in prison. (Please note that this is a minimum security facility)

Answer (TJ)-

4:30 a.m. Up for breakfast that is if you signed up for it. One of the Correctional Officers (CO) would come by and either knocks on your cell or shine a flashlight on you to awaken you. We had to count by 2's to go to the chow hall. Regardless how the weather elements were-we walked 2 by 2 while the CO's rode in the van. Whether it was snow or ice we walked with our 'unlined' jackets to get our meals. If someone stepped out of line, some of the CO's would stop the line and hold up the entire line as punishment. It could be snowing or raining—it didn't matter, we stood still until that CO was satisfied, and then we could then proceed to the chow hall.

5:00 a.m. - While in the chow hall we only had 5 -10 minutes to actually eat. The Lieutenants worked the actual chow hall. There were signs on the wall "Duck when shots are fired". While we are yet eating counts of the tables were done. Whether you finished or not after the 10 minutes we stood paired back up 2 x 2 and walked back to our units.

7:00 a.m. First shift C.O.'s –we were counted again and you had to be on your assigned bunk at 7:00.

8:00 a.m. Whatever assignment you had—work or school or to the yard outside—you must sign out to go to wherever place that you were permitted to go. The Majors run the shifts. Before leaving your unit—you had to sign out.

11:00 a.m. Count time before lunch. Again same routine line up 2 x 2 straight lines no talking.

3:00 p.m. Shift change—count time when 2nd shift CO's arrive.

7:00 p.m. Count time before supper. Same routine-line up 2 x2 straight lines no talking. At meal times you sat with the guys from your unit-whomever you were in line with that is whom you sat beside. No such thing as choice seating.

10:00 p.m. Your day was basically over—you had to be in your cell for count time. You could read, or watch TV-but everybody was counted again at 10:00 p.m. Now depending on whom your cell mates were would determine how long you kept the lights on in your cell. The cell mate (referred to as celli) who had the most seniority in the joint dictated whether your lights went out at 10:00 or later. Respecting the hierarchy in prison can save an inmate lot of grief. Prison is not the place where a newbie comes to try to blow himself up—just follow the rules and do your time.

Question: What was the overall atmosphere like inside your block- was it full of depression or was there any hope or anything remotely positive?

Answer (TJ) - Well the atmosphere changed when the inmates changed. Sometimes it was volatile-it was nothing to hear mother####r or nig####r. You had to handle yourself because everybody was watching to see if you would punk out. The young boys didn't really care –most were from the South Side of Chicago and they would tell you that they didn't care. This would depress you because the fellows didn't care. We would sit there watching television and saw some guys who had just been released who were now on the WGN news. Some had gotten killed after release and some would come right back in. This is what's referred to as the revolving door. I saw many guys come and go back in and out. I was determined to do my three years and never return to this joint or any other penal institution. There were murderers in the joint on very light drug charges and some appeared positive but it was still depressing. We slept in a 3 man cell with 3 bunks. The newbie got the top bunk-of course. I was housed in building called the 'castle' located on top of the hill with dormitories. There was no air conditioning and hot as a 'mug'. I struggled with

ONE ON ONE INTERVIEW WITH MY SON, THE FORMER INMATE (FI)

my asthma not having air conditioning. We were allowed to have televisions which had to be purchased from the state. During my last year in prison, I was moved (promoted) to the honor dorm. It had air conditioning and there were no cells but we had brick cubicles. I felt like the Jefferson's, I had moved on up!!

Question: What about the correctional officers (CO's)? I've seen documentaries on Lockup on MSNBC plus I was on my church's prison ministry team and we had some interaction with the officers?

Answer (TJ) - A few of them were a___holes-they actually took their jobs to the extreme. Heck I knew I had been sentenced to 6 years but did the CO's have to treat me subhuman like an animal. They would search your rooms everyday for no reason tossed your belongings on the floor actually tore up your cell and of course every time that tore up your cell, you had to put it back together. I saw this as borderline harassment. Not one time in our cell did they locate any contraband. One time a CO went through my photo album, my mom would send me lots of pictures and my son's mother would occasionally send some pictures. The CO went through my album tossed the pictures on the floor and then walk on your 'sh##'. That really made me mad but you couldn't say anything and you had to be careful about facial responses for fear of being written up and tossed in solitary confinement. What I witnessed was that some of the CO's -not all of them would try to provoke you to anger and hope that you would step out of line and make that fatal mistake of hitting one of them. If you hit or attacked a CO you would be sent to the Super Max prison in southern Illinois and it is underground—called TAMMS. The young CO's were cool they did their jobs without being on a power trip.

Question: What about the Statesville Prison experience—which can be viewed as the clearing house for all new coming inmates.

Answer (TJ) - Nearly all the correctional officers (CO's) were black and several displayed ghetto mania to the fullest degree. They talked down to all of us. All types of inmates were housed at Statesville, which is a very old institution. I almost felt as though I was in the jungle. Some inmates would actually shake their private parts at the CO's and at newcomers who were being brought in. I wondered—what the hell have I gotten myself into? Now this is the first stop after I left the Peoria County Jail after being sentenced. This was a very bad place. We could only shower weekly and the showers were rolled around on wheels—yes, the shower was on wheels. The inmates were cruel and so were the CO's. The most demeaning time of my entire prison sentence was what all transferees who were being shipped out from Statesville had to go through. They put us all in a fenced holding pen which held about 300 men and we all had to strip naked. This was so much like being on a slave ship during the movies 'ROOTS' or 'AMISTAD." I guess the CO's wanted to make sure that we did not have anything on us before being shipped by bus to our next home for however many years that we were sentenced to. Each bus held 60 inmates and again 95% of those on the bus were black. It felt like we were cattle on the bus. We were handcuffed at the ankles and wrists. There was no toilet on the bus only a paint bucket. It really makes you swallow your pride. I remember it was around 5:00 a.m. when we boarded the bus from Statesville. It took 24 hours to drop off and empty a bus of 60 inmates. The CO's drove the buses and that extra driving time meant overtime pay for them. At every drop off, there were guns pointed at you. There was no air conditioning on the bus and all the windows were painted so you didn't know where you were headed to. You were given a sack lunch which included apples and a peanut butter sandwich and milk—knowing well this was a recipe for unwanted bowel movements and body gas with no toilet.

There was no fighting on the bus and it would have been hard to fight anyway you were handcuffed and had on leg shackles to there was no movement at all on the transporting bus. On the entire trip I could not believe that this was happening to me. I thought about my year old son and my mother the entire trip—shaking my head (not outwardly of course) angry at myself for getting in this predicament.

ONE ON ONE INTERVIEW WITH MY SON, THE FORMER INMATE (FI)

I begin to think to myself, surely all the bad guys couldn't be black –however out of a busload of inmates, at least 45 were black. I know, as God is my witness, that we were not the only ones breaking the law—it was clear to me as I sat my a## on the bus, that the white guys were catching all the breaks.

Question: How have you explained to your son now almost ten years old why you were gone out of his life for 3 years?

Answer (TJ) - My son understands that dad got into trouble and had to go to jail. I told him that these people are not playing with you-so "Stay out of Trouble". Even though I put myself into that situation, I feel that my sentence could have been suspended. My first offense and nobody got hurt and even the judge himself said he hated that he had to give me any time. I no longer believe in the system and it is getting even harder to continue to believe in this country. I don't feel that the judge exercised his authority over the recommended sentence from the District Attorney.

Question: What kept you going on the inside for those 3 years?

Answer (TJ) - Teddy Bear (my son). I have been through a lot and have seen a lot of bad stuff. The point that I want to prove to my haters and to myself is that "I'm still standing". The crime I committed is not who I am. I remember when I was 16 years old and was at the shopping mall I innocently gave a guy a ride to the South side of the city and was rushed by him and his boys who pulled a gun on me. Like a typical teenager my gas gauge was on 'E' so I told them that I needed to stop and get a couple of dollars of gas which was my opportunity to get away. I went inside and asked the clerk to call the police—the boys came in to try to rob the place and pull me out-I fought to break away and the police came just in time and arrested them. Thank God for the cameras in the store. This proved that I was the kidnapped victim. For some reason my mind flashed back to that event and I do not want my son to go through anything like that when he is a teenager. While on the inside, some of the inmates' families abandoned them—so much that the inmates became hard as a rock and most developed a 'don't care attitude'. Letters from my mom and my maternal grandmother came every other week and in those letters and cards they would inform me how much money that had enclosed to be put on the 'books' for me. I received pictures of my son from his mother. My mom also sent me local newspaper articles, magazines, paperback books and of course the men's bible. I called my mom and grandmother twice monthly-the collect calls from prison were very expensive which is why they asked me not to call weekly but every other week. This correspondence from family was one of the main reasons for me not losing my sanity while incarcerated. Fast forward to today-the crime I committed is not who I am.

Question: What was your lowest point while on the inside?

Answer (TJ) - The time when I did not hear from my friends and my baby's mama to know where my son was. For months at a time everybody went silent-with the exception of my immediate family. Friends who said they were going to stick by you got real quiet and it hits you-Wow- they really don't care like they said they did—I'm thinking I had love and I guess I really didn't. So I was exposed to 3 years of mostly ignorant conversation and before long it began to rub off on me. I am so glad my mother sent books to me to help keep my mind elevated and focused. The old timers on the inside would remind me 'Never forget where you are'—there were prison gangs inside whose rank and file showed their shot callers' ultimate honor in all races. I did make some 'friends' on the inside. Because of my quiet demeanor and boyish face a lot of the guys wondered why was I in there and even some told me "man, you do not belong in here".

Question: What has been your lowest point since being back on the outside?

Answer (TJ) - Once people find out that you've done time in prison or jail-they start judging you. There are certain apartments that I cannot live in because I have a felon, cannot live in public housing, certain professions and jobs that are off limits because of my background. No matter where I go even when I get to be 50 years old, I will still be known as an ex- felon. This is very depressing as if I walk around branded 'F' for felon for life.

Question: How do you see yourself today, you're now 34 years old—what's your plan?

Answer (TJ)—Man that's a whole lot in that question. First of all, I do take ownership of my mistake. I acted foolishly and got convicted and did my time inside and on paper. I now take life more seriously and I look at every situation from different angles. I want to go back to school before I'm too old but this part-time job I've held for 1 and ½ years pays the bills and now I have medical benefits and can get paid time off. I want to eventually relocate back to Illinois to be closer to my son before he becomes a teenager, for those are difficult years for any young boy whose dad is not in the house or nearby.

Question: What would you like to tell America-the public and any future employers about Former Inmates struggle to find a job?

Answer (TJ) - I really think that former inmates get a bad rap. Judge me by 'my worth' and not by what is said on a piece of paper of what I did. And don't shut the door so fast. Let the former inmate (FI) express himself and give him (her) a chance to prove themselves on the job. Define me as a person and not as a background check. Now I'm not naïve enough to think that every person who walks out of jail or prison wants a job and wants a new start. Based on what I've seen on the inside—if a person doesn't have a support system in place when they walk out—they are more than likely going to join the group of Former Inmates who come back through that revolving door. Additionally because of funding cuts in the states—there was hardly any rehabilitation in the prison. A lot of guys just sit around did their time with no mental stimulation at all and these guys are expected to come out and compete in the job market? One of my good friend's dad (who's in his fifties) just got charged and arrested for molesting his own children. The police and judge took the word of a wife (who happens to be white) and who is a crack head. When this dad gets out (he'll be in his 70"s)—my friend will have to take care of him. He loves his kids so the family is thinking that the 'racial' divide reared its ugly head again and they were actually married—not strangers.

Question: As you look back on how you went from delivering pizzas one moment to being put in the back of a squad car the next moment- what advice do you have for young 20 year olds coming behind you?

It's not always about the ladies—plan your work and work your plan. Life is moving on-one bad evening can change your life forever. If you act irresponsibly and too quickly without thinking -- guess what there's a cell waiting for you and 5-6 digit number waiting to replace your real name. Finish your education. Don't fall into 'another black man off the street' syndrome. Focus—start your own business-- keep your life on track. I took a detour but I'm working hard to get back on track. There are new prisons being built every day—so where are they going to get the people to fill them up?? You got it—one small slip up and you'll end up in your state run bed and breakfast with bars and no freedom. Stop; think about what you're doing or about what you're "thinking" about doing. Life is better on the outside than on the inside. Trust me –I know personally.

Question: Most statistics say that if a young black man doesn't have a father in the home, he will most likely end up in jail. Your father was in the home married to your mother—what happened?

Answer (TJ) - Just because a father is in the house-doesn't mean that there was a relationship intact. I come from a small family –I have one brother but my family is not close. I'm closer to my mother than I am to my dad—so is my baby brother. My brother is an attorney and he and I are not very close. I did not get any fatherly wisdom from my

ONE ON ONE INTERVIEW WITH MY SON, THE FORMER INMATE (FI)

dad-we did not have the sex talk. I don't blame him for what I did. I'm just saying perhaps if there were a stronger relationship between us, his voice of reason just might would have resonated within me as I was taking the wrong turn in life that landed me in the state prison for 3 years. My dad never questioned my friends or the people I hung out with—it was always my mom asking me who were the parents of such and such and where do they live. In my case the statisticians are dead wrong—I am the EXCEPTION. My parents are both college graduates, they didn't and still do not use drugs, they're both hard working and even still I ended up in prison. I am also the exception because I think I heard in some report that the majority of the inmates especially the black ones did not finish high school nor have they obtained the GED—look I had almost 2 years of community college under my belt when this detour occurred. I guess what I'm saying is that regardless of the stock that you come from and what you were taught as a child—LIFE still HAPPENS. I made a bad decision and landed on the wrong side of the law.

As I had mentioned in the earlier part of this chapter, these were my son's own words, some were edited slightly, but I wanted you to experience just how he felt approximately 4 years after his release. If you have a loved one who has recently been released—give them a moment to process all that they've been through while on the inside of jail or prison, especially if theirs was as my son's was—the first time(and hopefully the last time) being locked up. Everybody adjusts differently. I, as his mother, will probably never know all that my son went through while locked in a state prison for 3 years. I am glad that my prayers helped sustained him along with a longing desire to once again hold his own son.

***I am the Mother of a Prisoner, and this is my Story*.**

DEAR SON
(Response to Interview)

THIS CHAPTER IS written to my son in response to the interview in the previous chapter in which he opened up and poured out of his heart as he allowed me, his mother, yet in this situation, the author, to do a formal interview about his prison experience. I pause now to challenge each person reading my story to dare do a formal interview with your loved one about their prison experience. It will be very hard to keep your eyes dry at the same time wondering where I went wrong to contribute to my own son (or daughter) to ending up in prison.

It was the evening after Memorial Day 2013 when you came by as agreed and allowed me to question you for about two hours about the whole experience. I thought I was ready for it, but to say the least, it was very difficult. Your language was raw at times, but you would always back up and show respect for me when profane words or phrases would come up and eventually come out.

Son, as you spoke I listened intently and saw me "in you" as you spoke. Here you sit, my own offspring, with my own DNA, telling me, the author, of the hell you went through while incarcerated. I wanted to hug you every time when I saw the anger and disgust rise up in your spirit. I saw you two-fold, as my little boy who always had a deep voice (even before puberty) and now as a grown man. Internally, I was saying "Mama's here now and everything will be

DEAR SON (RESPONSE TO INTERVIEW)

alright". My favorite line to you is that you've got my DNA and personality so I know what's in you. Spoken like a true mother right?

Dear Son, I am sorry that you got caught up in this sometimes unfair judicial system. Your dad and I tried very hard to shield you and your brother from the ugly ways of the world that we live in. Your actions did however put you front and center as the face of the incarcerated.

Dear Son, I taught you the Word of God at an early age and you have seen the hand of God at work in our very lives. Do you remember the proclamation that the Lord impressed upon me to draft the Christmas of 2001 acknowledging that we are not an ordinary family and that we have been chosen by the eyes of the Lord to show Himself strong on our behalf? Remember every family member signed that as a Christmas gift to Jesus—well the Lord saw you sign that, and He did and still is showing Himself strong on all our behalf. Remember that you were facing 30 years for your offense (blunder) but the Lord moved upon the judge and you were sentenced to 6 years but did only 3. My continued encouragement to you was the fact that you were in the 'transformation chamber'-so let God change you. You made a mistake, you took a detour but God still loves you. The Lord knew in 2001 when we signed our family proclamation those 3 years later (2004) your dad and I would move to Texas and 5 years later (2006) that you would be sitting in a prison cell. Something this horrendous could have destroyed our family had we not been undergirded in and by prayer.

Dear Son, I never imagined that all the years that I was serving on the church's prison ministry teams that one day my 'own' son would end up in that place.(not the same facility) The Lord knew then, but I did not. I was just being faithful to what I believe was my calling. My heart went out to all the brethren who were in those 2 Illinois facilities who yet found time to come to chapel services for years to get strength and encouragement. My compassion was so real (and still is) that I believe because of the labor of love with the prison team—God used that time as seed sown to reduce your original sentence time. I honestly believe that. Thank you, Jesus.

Dear Son, I want you to know that many men which are jailed/imprisoned (some unjustly) have come out and redirected their lives to become leaders and role models such as President Nelson Mandela, Rev.Dr. Martin Luther King, Jr., Illinois Congressman Bobby Rush, Rev. Jessie Jackson, Judge Greg Mathis and countless others.

Dear Son, I charge you to hold your head up high, you've done your time, you've completed your parole, as an Indentured servant, and now it's time to Move Forward. Our life's experiences mold us into whom we will eventually become.

Know this, that God is not through with you yet. Dare to make lemonade out of those 3 lemon years behind bars away from your family and your son. You took ownership of your wrongdoing; it is time to move on.

Dear Son, I thought about you every day while you were away, never forgot your birthdays. It was especially hard without you at Thanksgiving and Christmas. I would sit and wonder how you were celebrating these sacred holidays behind the fence looking at a gray wall away from your family.

Dear Son, we love you, we support you, we forgive you for your actions, and we forgive you for putting your family through this ordeal now it's time for you to forgive yourself.

Dear Son, by the Grace of God-you got through it, now what?

Dear Son, please repeat after me: I am not what my arrest record says I am. I am not what my sentence said I am. I am not what that six digit R57102 inmate number referred to me as. I am Who God says I am. I can have what God says I can have. If any man be in Christ, he is a new creature. I am a new creature and I am Moving Forward.

I am the Mother of a Prisoner and this is my story.

WHERE DO WE GO FROM HERE –IT'S NOT YOUR FAULT

I AM TRULY grateful that my son is no longer in prison. How does he make up for those three years on the inside and the three very restrictive years on the outside-a total of six years of being on the radar of the Department of Corrections System? What about those years being away from his young son? No one brings their newborn child home from the hospital with the thought of him or her one day ending up on the wrong side of the justice system. No one watches their son or daughter march across the stage at graduation and embraces the possibility that their child could one day end up in a 7 x 9 cell.

In life things happen. You get through it with God's grace and knowing that if your child ends up 'Behind the Fence'- "It Is Not Your Fault". I want to make a distinction about my last comment. If you, as a parent or guardian, have done all that is within your power to provide a home for them, food and clothing, and you have even exposed them to positive activities that will help mold them into responsible adults- "It is not your fault" if they end up on the wrong side. If you corrected or disciplined them in some way when they did something wrong, "It is not your fault". If you gave them your attention when they needed it and always gave them your heart, "It is not your fault". If you made sure they went to school, met their teachers, reviewed their homework and gave them a scheduled bed time, then "It's not your fault." If after all of the previous scenarios, plus nurturing and showing love to your child, and he(she) still ends up in prison, it is definitely" not your fault". Now here comes the distinction(s): if you did drugs, drank alcohol around and sometimes with your child, the lines of parenting may have gotten a bit blurred. If you constantly showed your child disregard of the law, showed them how not to be a good neighbor, and even ignored your child's needs, you must own your part of laying the foundation for your child 'possibly' going wayward and ending up with the wrong crowd. There is no perfect formula of prison proofing your child because again I say- in life Things Happen.

This latter group of people or perhaps just one individual, in my opinion, did everything short of turning the key and unlocking the door to the jail for their son or daughter. We cannot choose our child's friends. I personally tried this. It did not work. The fact is that most children strive to emulate the continued example which is set before them, be it good or bad, positive or negative. Have you ever met a parent who scolded their child by saying (in their own way) "do as I say and not as I do"? Know this one thing; you are not solely responsible for your child's misjudgments in life. Every human being has a brain which is wired to take each of us to the moon mentally, if we dare use it, make demands of it and feed it with the proper nutrition internal and external.

As you are nearing the close of my story, remember that my son was in his early twenties when he took a wrong turn and let his emotions dictate a bad decision by him. I don't know under what circumstances that your child or relative took a detour, but I'm here to tell you that there is a road back. Your child will need you even more after release, on this road back.

Even if you know someone's child or relative who has been sentenced to a much longer time than my son, there is still a road back. In such an instance, affirmations plus motivations coupled with attending chapel service at that facility will definitely add to your child's

WHERE DO WE GO FROM HERE –IT'S NOT YOUR FAULT

inner strength-which is a key component of doing jail/prison time.

I told my son regularly in my letters to him, that" while you're in this' Transformation Chamber' (jail/prison), let the Lord transform you." A few coy remarks from other people do trouble me from time to time especially from well known radio personalities. One in particular is when people poke fun at inmates that proclaim to have 'found Jesus' while incarcerated. Here is the overlooked memo about this 'jab'– Jesus was not lost. My son stated to me that when it became clear to him that this little spat between he and his girlfriend had suddenly (in his mind) become serious felony charges which caused him to be bound in shackles both hands and feet, he did call on Jesus.

It is not because my son was in prison that I am bothered by those types of comments, I think they are just ugly and damnable. Out of the abundance of the heart, the mouth will surely speak. If you ever want to know what's in a person's heart, just listen at what they spend the most of their time speaking about. That is the gauge-what's in the heart comes out through the mouth. He also said when he heard that jail door being slammed behind him, the only person he could call on was Jesus. I believe that when silly uninformed people with or without a microphone take those cheap shots at a personal declaration, it shows how small they really are. I dare them to "walk a mile in my shoes." There are many people in our society who are bent on criminalizing parents and other family members because of the action of the incarcerated loved one.

It took the love of Jesus to comfort my son every night and to protect him from those people on the inside who have nothing to lose by doing harm to him or any other inmate. It took the whispers of the Holy Ghost to help my son take ownership of his offense and yet believe with God's help he could do his sentencing time and not crack under the pressure and cruelty of prison confinement. Amen! I also searched within myself, as a mother, to see whether I did something which could have caused my son to ultimately end up in a state prison. After honestly examining the kind of parent I was and what I had taught both of my sons-I can honestly say that 'It was not my fault".

I remember during my years of prison ministry, several of the men confessed that their very lives had been spared by being sent to prison. What I gleamed from those statements was that they were involved in so much illegal activity and wrongdoings with and against other people that it was actually safer for them on the inside of the fence versus being on the outside.

In life, things do happen. My family got blindsided by this experience; but with the Lord's help we got through it and at the time of this writing, we are still getting through it. My son is a full grown man with a grade school aged son of his own. There were times when I found myself comparing the life of my now formerly incarcerated thirty-four year old son with that of his former classmates from Illinois and with other persons of his same age. Go ahead and say it –'that's not fair'. How could I make such a comparison? Well I never admitted it out loud until now. It sounds like an oxymoron, my son was in prison and I feel so bad that I'm assuming responsibility for it? Sorry if this statement really sounds like a prisoner's mother, because it is.

However it is not my fault. I will continue to be a support for my son. If he continues to frustrate himself over how could he have been so foolish to have messed up his life?

I will remind him again and again that taking a detour does not mean that you will not make it to your destiny; it merely means that it may take you a bit longer to get there.

I will keep encouraging him to rebrand himself by taking more educational courses, expanding his reading, writing down his goals and continuing to put one foot in front of the other. He has no reason to walk with his head down. He committed an offense, did his time and is trying to rebuild his life. My son currently has a part time job in the rehabilitative services field. It pays the bills, and he works the shifts that no one else wants to work. As a mother I will be there if he falls down again to help him back up and to let him know that it's alright to fall, but you must always, always get back up. What happened to my son in 2006 when he entered the state prison system is a chapter in his life and a chapter in mine. This incident does not define him, nor will I let it define me. Where do we go from here? We turn the page and keep moving forward. Everybody reading this book has a past, we all do. The only way that your past can catch up with you and overcome you is if you stop moving and remain in the idle gear too long. Where do we go from here? I will join the fight to do what I can to help restore the right to vote of former incarcerated individuals. Every state has their own requirements for ex-felons to vote. In a few states, that right is unfortunately lost forever. Former inmates are constituents and have families also. Their political voices been unfairly silenced far too long. They are still citizens of this great country, regardless of what a segment of society thinks.

Perhaps they took a detour just like my son, but after a debt to society has been paid where is the redemption? It is in their right to vote. I will continue to encourage as many former and current prisoners that despite their past offenses they still have value, not only to their families, but to the world itself. I believe that everybody in this world has a contribution to make no matter how small or insignificant it may seem to them. Sometimes people need help in stirring up the gift within.

It is also my hope that by helping to strengthen and shape the inner lives of former prisoners, they would seize the moment to reclaim their lives and hit the reset button. If people in general would stop the condescending remarks and prohibitive actions toward former prisoners, this would be a weight off of anyone who has ever worn a number across their chest and been identified only as such and who sincerely wants change in their lives. If you continue to degrade a person, continually reminding them of their past mistakes and never once giving them an opportunity to take ownership of their mistakes and to begin again, then this vicious cycle of hopelessness will continue.

In the six plus decades of my being on this earth, I have read about a lot of grotesque, savage and heinous offenses that have been committed by accused individuals. That person (criminal) still has a mother and that mother is probably shocked that her own offspring has stooped to the lowest degree of humanity by taking another person's life or whatever the atrocious offense was. It was not my intent as I stated earlier to romanticize my son's offense or any offense committed by any individual. God alone is the ultimate judge, but we are still a nation of laws and no one is above the law for his or her actions.

Because mothers are in fact the gateway by which we all enter the earth, is the basis for the extra closeness, the bond, if you will, between children and their mother. Of course there are some exceptions to every rule, including this one. It is out of that bond which gave me the authority to pen this memoir with such depth and transparency. It goes without saying the vital role which fathers also play in a child's life.

It is my hope that this book, Mother of a Prisoner, has enlightened your understanding, expanded your thinking and incorporated the role of our judicial system in the lives of many Americans. Hopefully America will one day surrender the title of being the Great Incarcerator. The United States of America makes up only 5% of the world's population and yet we represent 25% of the world's incarcerated population. It costs us more to incarcerate persons that it does to send them to college. Incarceration should not remain a big time employment business; let's work together on changing people from the Inside Out. Time will not allow speaking on the increase of private 'for profit' prisons in this country which some treat as an 'investment'—just like a stock asset. This trend is troubling in itself because stockholders would be pushing for greater occupancy within the prisons to increase the revenue stream on their financial statements. Just where do you think those extra occupants will come from and some most likely received harsher sentences than the offense carries all for the sake on keeping the bed count high in the for profit prisons. Prison reform is greatly needed.

Where do we go from here as a nation? We can do better. When I reached out for support for my son back in 2006, I never said that my son was innocent of his charges. In recent years, there have been way too may killing of unarmed black and brown men, which in a lot of cases were who were not even given a chance to prove or disprove allegations lodged at them. This happened because a few officers tried, convicted and executed their own version of justice against these men. This is a travesty and is in itself worthy of a moral outcry. I believe those 'few' officers who acted as vigilante justice with badges need to be reprimanded and themselves brought to justice. Silence is still consent. No one should be allowed to stand in the position of authority and enact injustice upon anybody 'you' feel deserving. I am grateful that when my own son was arrested without incident in 2005, was given the opportunity to answer his charges and he did his time. Thanks to the thousands of police officers across the country that do the right thing every single day. It is unfortunate that there are some who unfairly target all police as ambassadors of bad will. My heart also goes out to the hundreds of mothers whose sons either died while in police custody; were shot in the back, body slammed, stomped and punched countless times while handcuffed; choked to death and many other egregious things that were done to them (on camera) by that same small group of officers. America, the blood of those men and some boys is crying out for justice. How can I demand justice for another nation and deny justice to my own citizens? Maybe someone will propose a National Day of Repentance. The bible states that a man who won't provide for his own is worse than an infidel. The world is watching America and taking note how we treat our citizens. We need to stop carrying and wielding our bibles and start living and doing what the bible says. For those who profess to be Christians, do you not know that your very lives, in some cases, are the only bibles that people read? Lawmakers begin their congressional sessions with prayer and then turn around and negate their own prayers by legislating laws that are economically hurtful to so many. People in wheelchairs are kicked out the halls of Congress, protestors are pepper sprayed and beaten. What is this? We can do so much better.

Where do we go from here? For one, our Department of Justice should present itself as that arm of the government which pledges allegiance and pursues liberty and justice for ALL Americans not just for a select few. God Bless America and May God Help America.

I am the Mother of a Prisoner and this is my story.

Mother of a Prisoner

RESOURCES AND REFERENCES

Resources:

Department of Justice Website

ACLU Map of State Felony Disfranchisement Laws

Texas Secretary of State Website

Progress Illinois

ASCA-Association of State Correctional Administrators

Council of State Government Justice Center

Re-Entry Policy Council

Population Reference Bureau

BBC News

ACLU Website

Whitehouse.Gov website

References Mentioned:

The New Jim Crow	book by Michelle Alexander
You Don't Live on My Street	poem by Dr. Rebera Elliott Foston

References Mentioned (cont'd):

Walk a Mile in My Shoes	song by Joe South
Baretta Show Theme Song	performed by Sammy Davis Jr. Written by Dave Grusin & Morgan Ames
Lockup on MSNBC	series documentary TV reality
Monk former TV	series starring Tony Shalube
Scared Straight	Documentary TV program
ABC Evening News	Topic "Inmate Trains Dog for Autistic boy"
Shakespeare's Play	Hamlet
Holy Bible	King James version
Roots TV Miniseries	From Alex Haley's Book 'Roots'
Gifted Hands	Book by Dr. Ben Carson
Song by James Brown	I'm Black and I'm Proud

ACKNOWLEDGEMENTS

THIS BOOK IS a personal testimony and the story of what my son's incarceration did to me as a mother, as well as to our family. I want to thank my son, T.J., for opening up to me about this unforeseen prison experience and allowing me to share it with the world. He did not think that his actions would land him in a state penitentiary for three years out his life and rob his toddler son of being without his daddy for three years. I am also grateful for my understanding husband of forty-one years, who sat quietly as I bounced chapter ideas off of him and who comforted me when special segments of the book would grip my heart and drive me to tears. Initially he was not sure that he wanted to open up this segment of our lives to the world. But as I continued to labor with this project, he did all within his power to assist me --from turning our master bedroom into my office, purchasing and rearranging bookshelves as I accumulated more books and even settling for very light dinner meals when he knew I was facing my own deadline and did not have time to cook.

Special thanks go to my friend Alicia, who despite her own challenges, spent hours reviewing chapters with me at the Dairy Queen; My BFF, Johnnie Mae, who would listen intently as I read chapters to her over the phone and who would tell me don't stop but keep on reading and coached me over the phone how to use a flash drive. To Daphne, who lent her ear and experience as a former case manager who often used her lunch time to read chapters and offer constructive suggestions, many thanks.

I cannot forget my own mother, Mrs. Alberta Lewis, who is still able to read quite well at the young age of eighty-four years old, who every month put money on her grandson's books even though she was on a fixed income. She would also regularly accept expensive collect phone calls from prison from her oldest grandson-my son.

A big thanks to all of the other cheerleaders that have poked and prodded me to get this book finished and published. You know who you are. I actually finished the book near the end of 2014 and it has taken this long for final touches, amidst personal illnesses, family issues and mostly deciding to bring the topic to a close. There is always something in the headlines weekly about incarceration and the criminal justice system.

Lastly , but definitely not least, I want to thank the Holy Spirit who helped bring items to my remembrance about this ordeal to include in this book and who would direct me to the right scriptures for support when I felt discouraged. It was indeed the still small voice which said 'tell your story, people need to hear it.'

I am the Mother of a Prisoner and this is my story.

ABOUT THE AUTHOR

GERALDINE MURRELL-GODFREY IS a native of northwest Louisiana and a graduate of Southern University in Baton Rouge. She is one of two children and the only person in her family to attend and graduate from college. From an early age and not able to identify her intellectual drive, she has always been an avid reader. At ten years old while walking to school with the other neighborhood children, Geraldine passed by a bright, vacant house which just lit up her spirit. That house was going to be hers. She was raised in what is called a shotgun house- two rooms, a small kitchen and bath straight through.

Geraldine thought about that freshly painted house throughout school that whole day. After school she ran home and told her parents "you have got to see this house". Who knew that this was the making of a future Realtor of the Year? The agent came from Shreveport, showed them the inside, wrote up the papers and the rest is history. This is the same home that her 84 year old mother still lives in today. Geraldine says she sold her first house at the age of 10 and the commission she received was a home twice the size of that shotgun house. It had a large country front porch, living room, dining room, kitchen, 2 bedrooms, a full bathroom and a large yard with a private driveway. Her family felt like the Jefferson's—they had "moved on up". Her self-proclaimed Type A personality was rooted and grew from there.

She remembers the time when she and her brother were able to go uptown to the Parish library and check out books. In comparison to their small neighborhood library (used only by the blacks) which was one large open room less than 200 square feet. The big parish library (used mostly by the whites at the time) did fascinate this teenager. Geraldine has said that since she didn't have an older sister, things of a female nature, she learned about in books. Neither of her parents finished high school, and the subject of what was happening to her teenage body was not to be discussed at all. That's where the parish library opened up her understanding and started her on the road to expanded imagination and an increased knowledge of life in general.

While at Southern University, she obtained a Bachelor of Science degree in Accounting, made the Deans' List and graduated with honors. Her first job out of college was at a Fortune 500 company in central Illinois afterwards came a marriage to her college sweetheart, three babies (not all at once), the loss of her first born, and a lengthy real estate career which climaxed in being selected the 1995 Realtor of the year at the local Board of Realtors. This was a moment in history as it was the first time that an African American Realtor had received this designation from that local board of realtors. Almost 2 decades later and due to some health issues which contributed to the waning of her love for the real estate business, is when she accepted a job offer from the local housing authority.

Geraldine knew nothing about this part of the housing business, but spiritually speaking she reasoned within herself that she had worked with people who had money (while in real estate) and now she was working with people who didn't have much money(subsidized housing clients), she then considered herself well rounded to be used greatly by God.

Geraldine Murrell-Godfrey is a former cost accounting analysis clerk, realtor, and broker, sales trainer, housing director, real estate development specialist, landlord, Sunday school teacher and superintendent, minister in training, prison team member, and most recently Toastmasters Club member. She is currently a Housing Counselor with the local housing agency and an aspiring author. These jobs and vocations make up her six decades of being on this earth.

ABOUT THE AUTHOR

When did she decide to become an author? Someone once said that in order to become a writer, you must first be a reader. She reads lots of memoirs and considers herself a news junkie. She has breaking news alerts on her cell phone, receives various newsletters and

Currently has 6 active magazine subscriptions which include Time, O Magazine, Fortune, Essence, Entrepreneur and Sports Illustrated for her son.

Geraldine identifies her first life changing event as the death of her first born darling daughter at age six and a half months, while in the care of a babysitter, who just happened to be white. She was only twenty-five years old at that time, married and was at work on her first job when she received the disturbing call from that babysitter. What could prepare a young mother for such a tragedy-especially when this baby had been dedicated to the Lord, so much so that she was affectionately named Dedekinna. This was supposed to be the context of Geraldine's first book, which is still on the inside of her soul, not yet penned. I think it is safe to say that this event over 35 years ago was the driving force of putting her experiences on paper.

Geraldine identifies her second life changing event as when she was sitting with her dying father at the VA hospital in Shreveport in 1994. She states that she held her father's hand all the way to death's door and she admitted seeing the light as her dad took his last breath. Geraldine was 41 years old at the time and well established in her faith, so much so she didn't scream out when her dad made his transition. She sat still for a few moments praying silently and then she went to get the nurse on duty.

The next unexpected life changing event was when her oldest son, who is the spitting image of her late father, was incarcerated for three years. She and her husband had already moved to Texas at this time so her son was alone in Illinois. Geraldine felt that this should not have happened to her family. The spectrums of feelings which she experienced are all on display in this book, her memoir, "Mother of a Prisoner".

Let this book move you, motivate you and expand your thinking.

MOTHER OF A PRISONER

Perhaps if you're ever drawn into a conversation involving a formerly incarcerated person or family member thereof, you will think about what Geraldine has shared on these pages—what life is/was like being the Mother of a Prisoner?

I am the Mother of a Prisoner and this is my story.

CPSIA information can be obtained
at www.ICGtesting.com
Printed in the USA
BVHW03s2325100718
521078BV00005B/123/P